GLUTEN-FREE
Food for the family

THE AUSTRALIAN Women's Weekly

GLUTEN-FREE
Food for the family

CONTENTS

ABOUT ALLERGIES	6
BREAKFAST	12
LUNCH	44
DINNER	82
SWEET	134
SPECIAL OCCASIONS	160
STAR INGREDIENTS	180
GLOSSARY	182
CONVERSION CHART	187
INDEX	188

ABOUT ALLERGIES

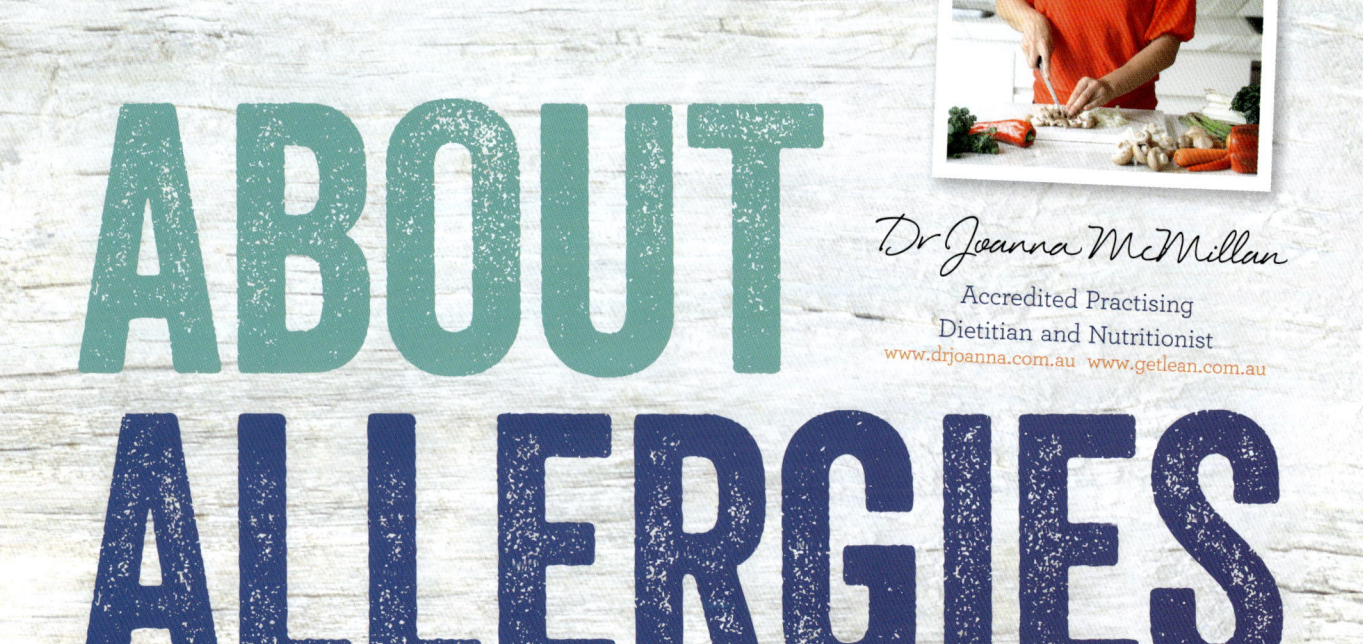

Dr Joanna McMillan
Accredited Practising
Dietitian and Nutritionist
www.drjoanna.com.au www.getlean.com.au

If you are picking up this book because you or a family member has a food allergy, you are not alone. The latest Australian data estimates that 1 in 10 infants have a food allergy, most commonly to **raw egg (8.8%)**, followed by **peanuts (3%)**, **cow's milk (2.7%)** and **sesame seed (0.8%)**. Fortunately, many grow out of their allergy in the first few years, leaving an estimated 3-5% of older children with an allergy. The food allergies a child is least likely to grow out of are peanuts, tree nuts, seeds and seafood.

If you have a young child with a food allergy, be sure to have an annual allergy review with your clinical immunologist. It makes life much easier to know if your child can now have egg, milk or whatever the offending food may be. Equally you both need to know if the allergy is potentially life-threatening.

In adults the rate is much lower, but there remains an estimated 1.3% who suffer from a food allergy.

The main offender is peanut, followed by prawn, cow's milk and egg. However, an allergy can develop at any time to pretty much any food. Allergies do not necessarily run in families; if one child has an allergy there is only a slight increase in risk of a sibling also having an allergy. Why some are affected while the majority are not, is a major question in allergy research, and there are not, as yet, any clear answers.

prosciutto-wrapped haloumi page 57

salmon and quinoa salad page 48

IS FOOD ALLERGY INCREASING?

Yes, it seems to be. In Australia, hospital admissions for severe allergic reactions have doubled over the last decade, and more people are seeking help from allergy clinics. This rise has been seen in the UK and USA, so we're not alone. Why this is happening is less clear. There are a number of hypotheses, but so far the research has not been able to provide any definitive conclusions. One theory is the 'hygiene hypothesis', which proposes that a lack of exposure to infections, germs, parasites and dirt in general in young childhood affects the development of the immune system. Another theory is the timing of introduction to solid foods. What is clear from the research is that delaying exposure to common allergens does not reduce the incidence of food allergy, and may even increase it. The latest Australian recommendations for infant feeding are to exclusively breastfeed to around 6 months, at which point solid foods, including potentially allergenic ones, should be introduced. We now have research to show that people who had a cat or dog at home during early childhood are significantly less likely to have a pet allergy later in life. The same may prove to be true of a food allergy. What is crucially important is that if you suspect a food allergy you seek the help of a health-care professional to confirm a diagnosis and help you to create a management care plan. Otherwise you may be unnecessarily restricting your own or your child's diet. With that comes a risk of missing out on specific nutrients, particularly if several foods are avoided. Another source of confusion is the difference between a food allergy and a food intolerance.

WHAT IS A FOOD INTOLERANCE?

The definition of a food intolerance is 'a reproducible, unpleasant (adverse), non-psychological reaction to a specific food or food ingredient'. In other words, the immune system is not involved. While many of the symptoms can be similar to a food allergy (although not as serious as an anaphylactic reaction), diagnosis can be much more difficult. This is due, in part, to the fact that symptoms can be delayed and may not appear until many hours after consuming the food.

For example, a common food intolerance is milk and is due to a lack of the enzyme lactase that breaks down the sugar (lactose) in milk. Without this enzyme the milk sugar enters the colon undigested where it is fermented by the resident bacteria, causing diarrhoea, discomfort and gas. This has a genetic link as people from Africa and Asia usually lack this enzyme whereas those of Caucasian origin are less likely to be affected.

Other common food intolerances are to wheat, dairy products, eggs, fish or shellfish, caffeine or soy products. The symptoms produced are similar to the less severe allergic reactions listed on the page opposite (page 9).

WHAT IS A FOOD ALLERGY?

Food allergy results when the immune system reacts to something in the food, usually a protein. The immune system is important in protecting us from disease, but when it reacts improperly to a food it can cause a variety of symptoms ranging from unpleasant to life threatening. In the most serious cases, anaphylactic shock occurs within a few minutes of exposure to the food. The symptoms include a swelling of the face, lips and tongue, weak pulse, dizziness and a difficulty in breathing. If this happens to your child, or you witness this response in someone else, you must seek medical assistance immediately.

This is the type of response that will occur in those with severe peanut allergy if they come into contact with peanut protein. This can be extremely difficult for parents as peanuts are used in many foods that you wouldn't expect. Children have reacted after eating a piece of birthday cake at a party or eating breakfast cereal that was packaged using the same machinery as a nut-containing variety. For this reason it is crucial that those with severe allergies wear an identification bracelet and carry an adrenaline autoinjector (epipen). Shellfish and bee stings are the other most likely candidates for such serious anaphylactic reactions.

With most food allergies, symptoms will appear within 30 minutes of consuming the food – this does have the benefit of making it easier to identify the allergen than is the case for food intolerances. What is important to note however, is that allergic reactions can escalate after the first or second exposures. It's therefore essential to develop an action plan with your clinical immunologist or allergist.

TYPICAL REACTIONS TO A FOOD ALLERGY OR INTOLERANCE

Reactions can affect four main areas:

- The gastrointestinal system: causing abdominal cramps, nausea, vomiting and/or diarrhoea. Nuts are often the culprit food where immediate effects take place. In chronic diarrhoea, most often in children, wheat, milk or soy products may be the cause.
- The skin: causing the eruption of hives or in some a swelling of the lips, ears, eyes and face. Eczema may also be due to a food allergy, but there are many other causes so it is important to seek proper medical advice before omitting foods from your or your child's diet.
- The respiratory system: causing a runny or stuffy nose. Although many people believe their asthma is linked to a food allergy, allergists consider this unlikely and airborne substances, such as dust mites, are the more likely offenders.
- The vascular system: causing a number of different symptoms from migraine headaches to numbness, flushing and dizziness. The latter may be caused by ingesting fairly large doses of mono-sodium glutamate (MSG) and is often referred to as Chinese restaurant syndrome due to their frequent use of this flavouring. However, the symptoms are short term and do not involve IgE (allergic) responses – the sign of a classic allergy. They don't require medical treatment and it usually just clears up on its own. So if someone suspects this is the case for them, avoiding excess MSG is wise. If you suffer from frequent migraines that cannot be explained by any other cause, you may benefit from experimenting with cutting out these foods from your diet: strong cheeses, red wine, champagne, chocolate, citrus fruit, gluten and cured meats such as bacon, salami, hot dogs and ham.

The difficulty with food allergies and intolerances is that they can be difficult to identify – the symptoms are usually non-specific and can be attributed to many other causes. Many people unnecessarily omit food from their diet believing they are intolerant to them (or have been told they are by those not qualified to do so). This may not be a problem if it is only one or two foods, but where these foods are not adequately replaced, or numerous foods are omitted, the individual is at risk of nutrient deficiencies.

Most commonly, people are advised to give up wheat and dairy products. This is not as easy as it sounds and, for the few individuals who are affected, the help of a dietitian is warranted to ensure the resulting diet is nutritionally sound. However, the vast majority of people do not need to give up these foods. Wheat and dairy foods have many benefits and need only be avoided by those with a true allergy or intolerance. The fact only 40% of people claiming to have a food intolerance actually show symptoms when tested is testament to the level of non-essential food restrictions we have placed on ourselves.

HOW DO YOU DIAGNOSE A FOOD ALLERGY OR INTOLERANCE?

The most common ways to test for a food allergy is with a skin test and/or a blood test. These must be carried out by a certified allergist/clinical immunologist as correct procedures must be followed to ensure the most accurate results.

The skin test uses a specially prepared extract of the suspect food, which is placed on the skin after the surface has been pricked, scratched or punctured. If a hive appears within 20 minutes, this shows that antibodies are present. The blood test (known as RAST) looks for antibodies directed against specific allergens, and can be used when skin testing is not practical due to severe eczema or hives. Both the skin and blood tests, however, can and do give false results. Many people who have a positive reaction to the tests may have no problems when they consume the food.

It is important, therefore, to discuss your results with a dietitian or doctor experienced in this area. Food intolerances can be far harder to pinpoint, and food challenges (eating the food thought to cause the problem) are often the only way to identify problem foods. This can be done yourself provided your symptoms are not severe, but it is best to do this under the guidance of a dietitian.

The first step is to keep a food diary and record any symptoms over a period of at least a couple of weeks. You can then start to identify if there is a pattern and consistent response after eating certain foods. One of the issues with intolerances, however, is that unlike an allergy, where you must avoid the offending food, intolerances usually have a threshold. You may be fine with a certain amount, but tip over the threshold and you experience symptoms. You may also be intolerant to a natural or added chemical in foods. This means many foods may be involved and so the cause can be increasingly difficult to identify. One food may tip you over the threshold but, in fact, many foods contributed in the lead up to the symptoms.

An experienced dietitian can help you navigate this process. You may go on an elimination diet that omits all suspect foods for at least a week. If symptoms persist you have either not eliminated the food or the problem does not lie with your diet. Once you are symptom free, you can re-introduce one food at a time over a 2-4 day period for each food. If symptoms re-appear you can correctly identify the offending food and cut it out of your diet. If many foods are involved, your dietitian will help you to plan an appropriate diet.

AVOID QUESTIONABLE TESTING METHODS

There are numerous companies and individuals cashing in on the current wave of media hype over food allergies and intolerances. The following are commonly used, but do not have scientific backing and are not approved by the Australasian Society of Clinical Immunology and Allergy (ASCIA):

- Sublingual food drops placed under the tongue
- Hair and nail analysis
- Pulse testing

- Cytotoxic food testing – uses an expensive blood test
- Kinesiologic testing – where your strength is measured before and after placing a small amount of test food under the tongue
- Iridology
- ALCAT testing
- Reflexology
- IgG antibody blood tests
- Vega testing
- Rinkel's intradermal skin testing

Many of these tests sound scientific, are usually expensive, and you end up with a long list of "to be avoided" foods that may be completely unnecessary. This can be harmful, particularly if the real cause of symptoms has not been correctly identified.

HOW TO MANAGE A FOOD ALLERGY

Better food labelling has made things easier for those living with a food allergy. There are now more foods than ever before on supermarket shelves that cater for specific food allergies. Learn what to look for in the ingredients list – in Australia the nine most common food allergens (peanut, tree nuts, milk, egg, fish, shellfish, wheat, sesame and soy) must be declared on the packaging. You'll usually find them in bold in the ingredients list. Imported food products must also comply with this labelling, but mistakes do happen. Be particularly careful with these products and read the labels carefully.

OUT AND ABOUT

Managing an allergy in the family is certainly easier at home where you can be more in control, but life has to happen and that means exposure to food at school, parties, visits to friends' houses and eating out. It's crucial that you give clear instructions to whoever is in charge at each of these venues. You may find it easier and safer to provide your own child's food in these instances.

Most primary schools and child-care centres are nut-free, but it is essential that you notify the school of any allergy that affects your child, including nuts. Mistakes do happen, and all it takes is your child to share a lunchbox item from a friend to be unwittingly exposed. Education of your child and those who care for them, in both avoiding the allergen and what to do in the face of a reaction, is essential.

Smart phone applications can make this process easier; there is now available at least one that allows you to pre-set your allergens or special diet and, on scanning the barcode on the food, will notify you immediately if it is safe for you to consume. This type of technology will continue to develop as more and more consumers demand and need to know exactly what is in their food.

FOR MORE HELP AND INFORMATION ON THIS TOPIC, HERE ARE SOME USEFUL WEBSITES
ASCIA *allergy.org.au* Food Intolerance Network *fedup.com.au* Allergy & Anaphylaxis Australia *allergyfacts.org.au*

BREAKFAST

BEFORE YOU START BASIC STEPS

HULLING STRAWBERRIES
The hull, or calyx, is the green leafy top of the strawberry. Cut around the leafy top and into the pale flesh underneath, then discard. Rinse the strawberries, then pat them dry with paper towel before using.

TRIMMING GREEN ONIONS
Pull the papery skin towards the root end of the onion, then remove and discard. Cut the roots off, then slice the white part of the onion as directed by the recipe. The green part can be used to garnish, either sliced or curled.

BREAKFAST

SLICING FENNEL

Use a V-slicer or mandoline to easily cut fennel into very thin, even slices. Simply slide the fennel back and forth across the blade. The adjustable blade is very sharp, so watch your fingers and use the guard supplied.

CHOPPING CHILLI

When cutting a chilli on the diagonal, leave it whole. The seeds are the heat source, so if you are not tolerant to high heat levels, remove the seeds and membranes first, or use less chilli.

BREAKFAST

GLUTEN FREE • DAIRY FREE • EGG FREE • NUT FREE

CINNAMON FUNNEL CAKES

PREP + COOK TIME 1¼ HOURS (+ STANDING) MAKES 24

You need a large piping bag fitted with a 1.5cm (¾-inch) plain piping tube and, if you have one, a sugar (candy) thermometer.

2½ cups (625ml) soy milk, warmed slightly

2 teaspoons (7g) dried yeast

2½ cups (335g) gluten-free self-raising flour

⅓ cup (75g) caster (superfine) sugar

vegetable oil, for deep frying

2 teaspoons ground cinnamon

2 tablespoons gluten-free icing sugar (pure confectioners' sugar)

1 Combine milk and yeast in a small bowl. Cover; stand in a warm place for 10 minutes or until frothy.
2 Whisk flour and sugar in a medium bowl. Make a well in the centre and pour in yeast mixture; mix until smooth. Cover bowl with plastic wrap; stand in a warm place for 30 minutes or until mixture rises slightly.
3 Heat oil in a large heavy-based saucepan over medium-high heat until oil reaches 150°C/300°F on a sugar thermometer (or when a cube of bread turns golden in about 30 seconds).
4 Whisk batter until smooth. Spoon mixture into piping bag; pipe 10cm (4-inch) diameter spirals of mixture into the hot oil. Deep fry on both sides until browned lightly. Drain on paper towel. Repeat with remaining mixture to make a total of 24 cakes.
5 Dust cakes with combined cinnamon and sifted icing sugar.

nutritional count per cake 3.1g total fat (0.4g saturated fat); 435kJ (104 cal); 17.5g carbohydrate; 1.4g protein; 0.1g fibre

tips You can use your favourite dairy-free milk for this recipe or, if you don't have a dairy allergy, use whichever milk you like. Instead of cinnamon sugar, you could drizzle the cakes with maple syrup, golden syrup, honey or warm chocolate ganache. Funnel cakes are best cooked just before serving.

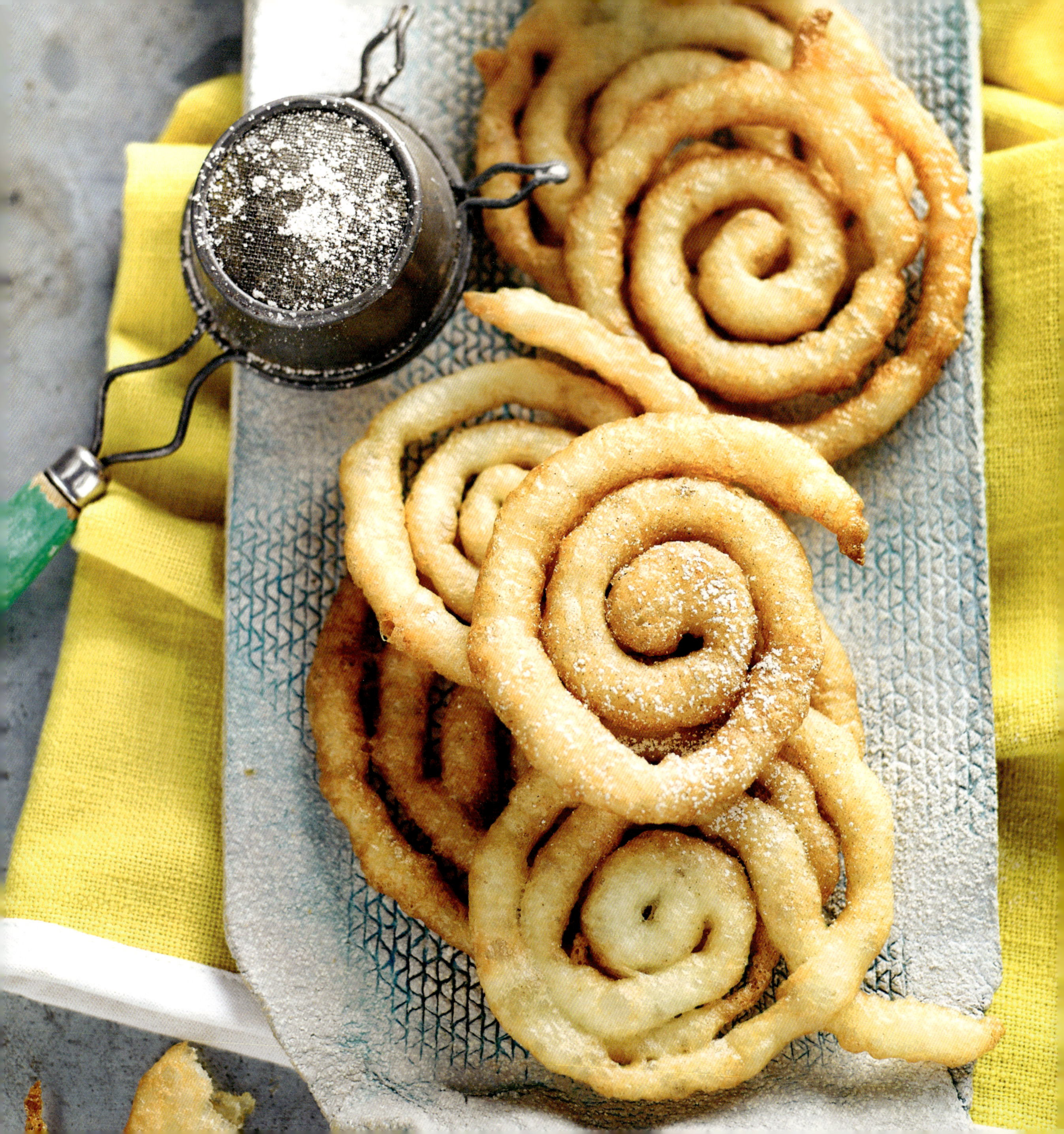

IF YOU DON'T HAVE A WAFFLE IRON, YOU CAN COOK THE WAFFLES IN A JAFFLE IRON. WAFFLES CAN BE FROZEN IN AN AIRTIGHT CONTAINER FOR UP TO 3 MONTHS; REHEAT IN A MODERATE OVEN FOR ABOUT 15 MINUTES OR UNTIL WARMED THROUGH. YOU CAN USE YOUR FAVOURITE DAIRY-FREE MILK IN THIS RECIPE.

GLUTEN FREE • DAIRY FREE • NUT FREE

BUCKWHEAT WAFFLES WITH GOLDEN SYRUP

PREP + COOK TIME 45 MINUTES SERVES 6

- ⅓ cup (60g) dairy-free spread
- 2 tablespoons caster (superfine) sugar
- 3 eggs, separated
- ⅓ cup (45g) gluten-free plain (all-purpose) flour
- ⅓ cup (50g) buckwheat flour
- ⅓ cup (50g) 100% corn (maize) cornflour (cornstarch)
- 1 cup (135g) gluten-free self-raising flour
- 1 teaspoon gluten-free baking powder
- 1 teaspoon bicarbonate of soda (baking soda)
- ½ teaspoon salt
- ½ teaspoon ground cinnamon
- 1½ cups (375ml) soy milk
- 1½ teaspoons white vinegar
- cooking-oil spray
- 250g (8 ounces) strawberries, sliced
- ⅔ cup (230g) golden syrup

1 Beat dairy-free spread and sugar in a medium bowl with an electric mixer until light and fluffy. Beat in egg yolks one at a time.
2 Beat egg whites in a small bowl with an electric mixer until soft peaks form. Gently fold egg whites into egg-yolk mixture.
3 Fold sifted dry ingredients, soy milk and vinegar into egg mixture until the mix just comes together. (Do not over mix the waffle mixture; it may look slightly curdled at this stage.)
4 Spray a heated waffle iron with oil; pour ½ cup batter over bottom element of waffle iron. Close iron; cook waffle about 3 minutes or until browned both sides and crisp. Transfer waffle to a plate; cover to keep warm.
5 Repeat step 4 to make a total of 6 waffles. Serve waffles with sliced strawberries and drizzled with golden syrup.

nutritional count per serving 11g total fat (2.5g saturated fat); 1669kJ (399 cal); 78.2g carbohydrate; 6.4g protein; 0.8g fibre

BREAKFAST

GLUTEN FREE • DAIRY FREE • EGG FREE • NUT FREE

HAM AND GREEN ONION FRITTERS

PREP + COOK TIME 20 MINUTES SERVES 4

250g (8 ounces) red grape tomatoes

1 teaspoon balsamic vinegar

1½ tablespoons olive oil

1 cup (135g) gluten-free self-raising flour

¾ cup (180ml) soy milk

250g (8 ounces) gluten-free shaved ham, chopped finely

4 green onions (scallions), sliced thinly

1 large avocado (320g), chopped coarsely

1 Preheat oven to 200°C/400°F.
2 Place tomatoes on an oven tray; drizzle with vinegar and 1 teaspoon of the oil. Season. Roast for 15 minutes or until tomatoes just soften.
3 Sift flour into a large bowl. Gradually add milk, in batches, stirring after each addition. Add ham and green onion; stir to combine. Season.
4 Heat remaining oil in a large non-stick frying pan over medium heat. Spoon ¼-cups of batter into pan; cook for 2½ minutes each side or until golden brown and cooked through. Repeat with remaining batter to make a total of eight fritters.
5 Serve fritters with avocado and roasted tomatoes.

nutritional count per serving 24.8g total fat (5.6g saturated fat); 1822kJ (435 cal); 31.5g carbohydrate; 20.1g protein

tips You can use your favourite dairy-free milk for this recipe or, if you don't have a dairy allergy, use whichever milk you like. Replace the ham with frozen peas or corn for a vegetarian option. You can make these fritters with regular self-raising flour if you don't have a gluten allergy, though you may need to use less milk.

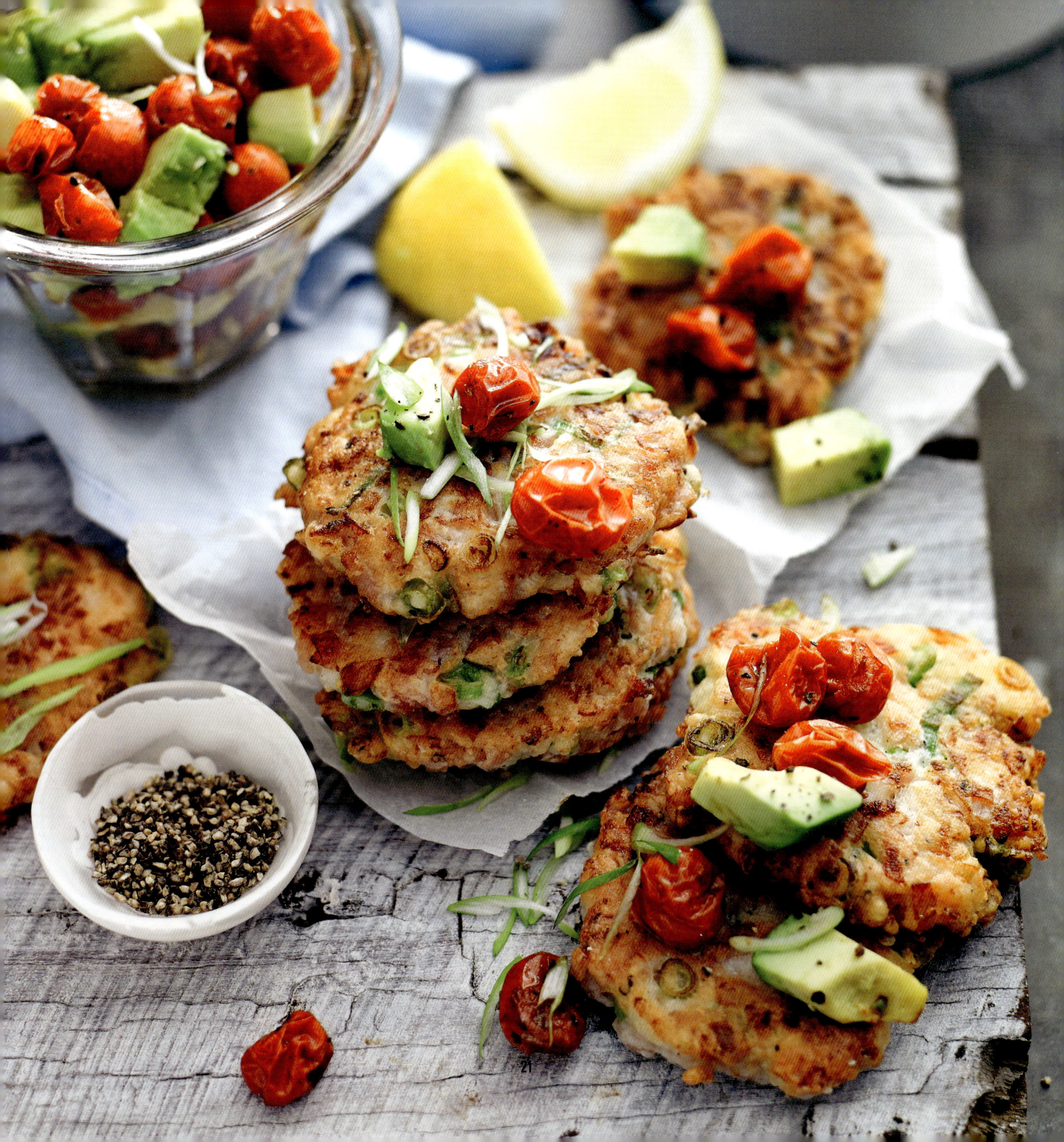

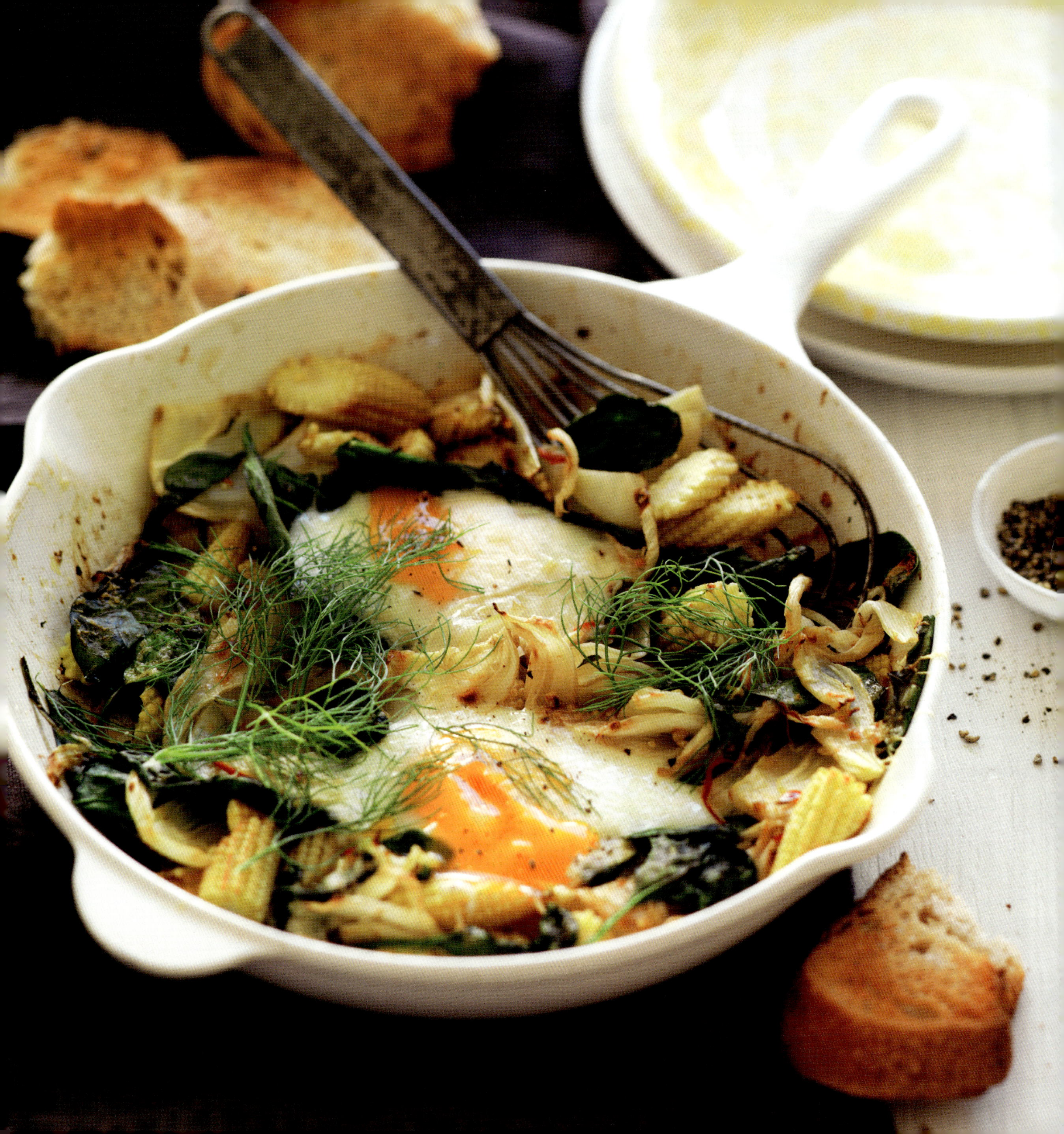

GLUTEN FREE • NUT FREE

GRILLED EGGS WITH SPICED FENNEL AND SPINACH

PREP + COOK TIME 20 MINUTES SERVES 4

You need an ovenproof frying pan for this recipe as the pan goes under the grill. If you don't have one, cover the pan handle with a few layers of foil to protect it from the heat.

1 tablespoon olive oil

1 clove garlic, crushed

1 fresh small red thai (serrano) chilli, sliced finely

1 small fennel bulb (200g), trimmed, sliced finely

200g (6½ ounces) baby corn, halved

100g (3 ounces) baby spinach leaves

4 eggs

2 tablespoon finely grated parmesan

4 slices gluten-free bread (180g), toasted

1 Preheat grill (broiler) to high.
2 Heat oil in a large ovenproof non-stick frying pan over medium heat; cook garlic, chilli, fennel and corn, stirring occasionally, for 5 minutes or until fennel is soft. Add spinach; cook, stirring, for 1 minute or until spinach has wilted.
3 Make four holes in the spinach mixture; break one egg into each hole. Sprinkle with parmesan.
4 Place under grill for 2 minutes or until eggs are cooked as desired.
5 Serve eggs and spinach mixture with toast.

nutritional count per serving 18.3g total fat (4.9g saturated fat); 581kJ (378 cal); 28g carbohydrate; 21.6g protein; 7.2g fibre

tips If you don't have a large enough frying pan to fit the four eggs, use two smaller pans. Reserve fennel fronds to scatter over eggs as a garnish.

BREAKFAST

GLUTEN FREE • YEAST FREE • NUT FREE

BUTTERMILK PANCAKES WITH LEMON AND SUGAR

PREP + COOK TIME 20 MINUTES SERVES 4

1 cup (135g) gluten-free self-raising flour
¼ cup (35g) gluten-free plain (all-purpose) flour
1 tablespoon caster (superfine) sugar
1 cup (250ml) buttermilk
½ cup (125ml) milk
2 eggs
20g (¾ ounce) butter, melted
½ cup (110g) caster (superfine) sugar
1 medium lemon (140g), cut into wedges

1 Sift flours and sugar into a medium bowl. Gradually whisk in combined buttermilk, milk and eggs until smooth. Stand for 5 minutes.
2 Heat a medium heavy-based frying pan over medium heat; brush with a little melted butter. Reduce heat to low, pour 2 tablespoons of batter into pan; cook until bubbles appear on the surface and top appears to dry out a little. Turn pancakes; cook until browned lightly. Remove from pan; cover to keep warm. Repeat with remaining butter and batter to make 12 pancakes, wiping out pan between batches.
3 Serve pancakes topped with sugar and lemon wedges.

nutritional count per serving 9.3g total fat (5.2g saturated fat); 1677kJ (401 cal); 72.3g carbohydrates; 7.7g protein; 0g fibre

MAKE PANCAKES JUST BEFORE SERVING.
SERVE PANCAKES WITH JAM AND CREAM, BUTTER AND
BROWN SUGAR, OR LEMON BUTTER, IF YOU LIKE.

GLUTEN FREE

QUINOA PORRIDGE WITH GRAPES AND PISTACHIOS

PREP + COOK TIME 25 MINUTES SERVES 4

Place 1 cup rinsed, drained white quinoa and 3 cups water in a large saucepan; bring to the boil. Reduce heat to low; cook, covered, for 10 minutes. Add 1 cup skim milk; cook, covered, for a further 5 minutes or until quinoa is tender. Stir in 2 medium coarsely grated pink lady apples and 100g (3 ounces) halved seedless red grapes. Serve porridge topped with another 100g halved seedless red grapes and ⅓ cup coarsely chopped toasted pistachios; drizzle with 2 tablespoons honey.

nutritional count per serving 8.9g total fat (1g saturated fat); 1642kJ (392 cal); 63g carbohydrate; 12.2g protein; 5.6g fibre

tip Most quinoa comes rinsed, but it's a good habit to rinse it yourself under cold water until the water runs clear, then drain it. This removes any remaining outer coating.

YOU CAN USE RED OR BLACK QUINOA FOR A BIT OF COLOUR; THE COOKING TIME WILL REMAIN THE SAME. YOU CAN USE YOUR FAVOURITE DAIRY-FREE MILK FOR THIS RECIPE OR, IF YOU DON'T HAVE A DAIRY ALLERGY, USE WHICHEVER MILK YOU LIKE.

GLUTEN FREE · DAIRY FREE · NUT FREE

QUINOA PORRIDGE WITH FIGS AND RASPBERRIES

PREP + COOK TIME 25 MINUTES **SERVES** 4

Place 1 cup rinsed, drained quinoa and 3 cups water in a large saucepan; bring to the boil. Reduce heat to low; cook, covered, for 15 minutes or until quinoa is almost tender and the water is absorbed. Add ½ cup soy milk, 2 tablespoons brown sugar and 1 teaspoon ground cinnamon; stir to combine. Cook for 5 minutes or until tender. Cut 2 fresh large figs into wedges. Serve porridge topped with figs and 150g (4½ ounces) fresh raspberries; drizzle with honey.

nutritional count per serving 3.8g total fat (0.5g saturated fat); 1192kJ (284 cal); 50.6g carbohydrate; 8.5g protein; 6.9g fibre

BREAKFAST

GLUTEN FREE • DAIRY FREE • YEAST FREE • NUT FREE

BREAKFAST WRAPS

PREP + COOK TIME 50 MINUTES MAKES 4

cooking-oil spray

4 eggs

4 rindless bacon slices (260g)

1 tablespoon dairy-free spread

150g (4½ ounces) button mushrooms, sliced thinly

60g (2 ounces) baby spinach leaves

2 tablespoons gluten-free barbecue sauce

GLUTEN-FREE WRAPS

2 eggs

1 cup (135g) gluten-free self-raising flour

⅓ cup (50g) buckwheat flour

⅓ cup (45g) gluten-free plain (all-purpose) flour

⅓ cup (50g) 100% corn (maize) cornflour (cornstarch)

1½ teaspoons salt

⅔ cup (160ml) soy milk

⅔ cup (160ml) water

1 Make gluten-free wraps.
2 Spray a medium frying pan with oil; cook eggs over medium heat. Transfer to a plate; cover to keep warm.
3 Cook bacon in the same pan until crisp; transfer to the plate, cover to keep warm. Melt dairy-free spread in same heated pan; cook mushrooms over medium heat for 5 minutes or until just softened.
4 Divide spinach, mushrooms and bacon between wraps; drizzle with barbecue sauce then top with egg. Season. Roll wraps to serve.

GLUTEN-FREE WRAPS Beat eggs in a small bowl with an electric mixer until thick and pale. Stir in the sifted dry ingredients, and the combined milk and water, alternately, stirring until just combined; do not over mix. Heat a flat sandwich press until light indicates it is ready to use; spray with oil. Pour ⅓ cup of mixture in a circle shape onto press; fully close lid and cook for 2 minutes or until golden brown. Transfer to a plate. Repeat to make a total of four wraps.

nutritional count per wrap 20.6g total fat (6.5g saturated fat); 2148kJ (513 cal); 66.6g carbohydrate; 26.1g protein; 1.4g fibre

tips You need a sandwich press with two flat elements. If you don't have one, spread ⅓ cup of batter into a circle shape in a heated large frying pan; cook both sides until brown and cooked through. Unfilled wraps can be made a day ahead; store in the fridge in an airtight container, or freeze for up to 3 months. Reheat wraps in a heated frying pan until warmed through.

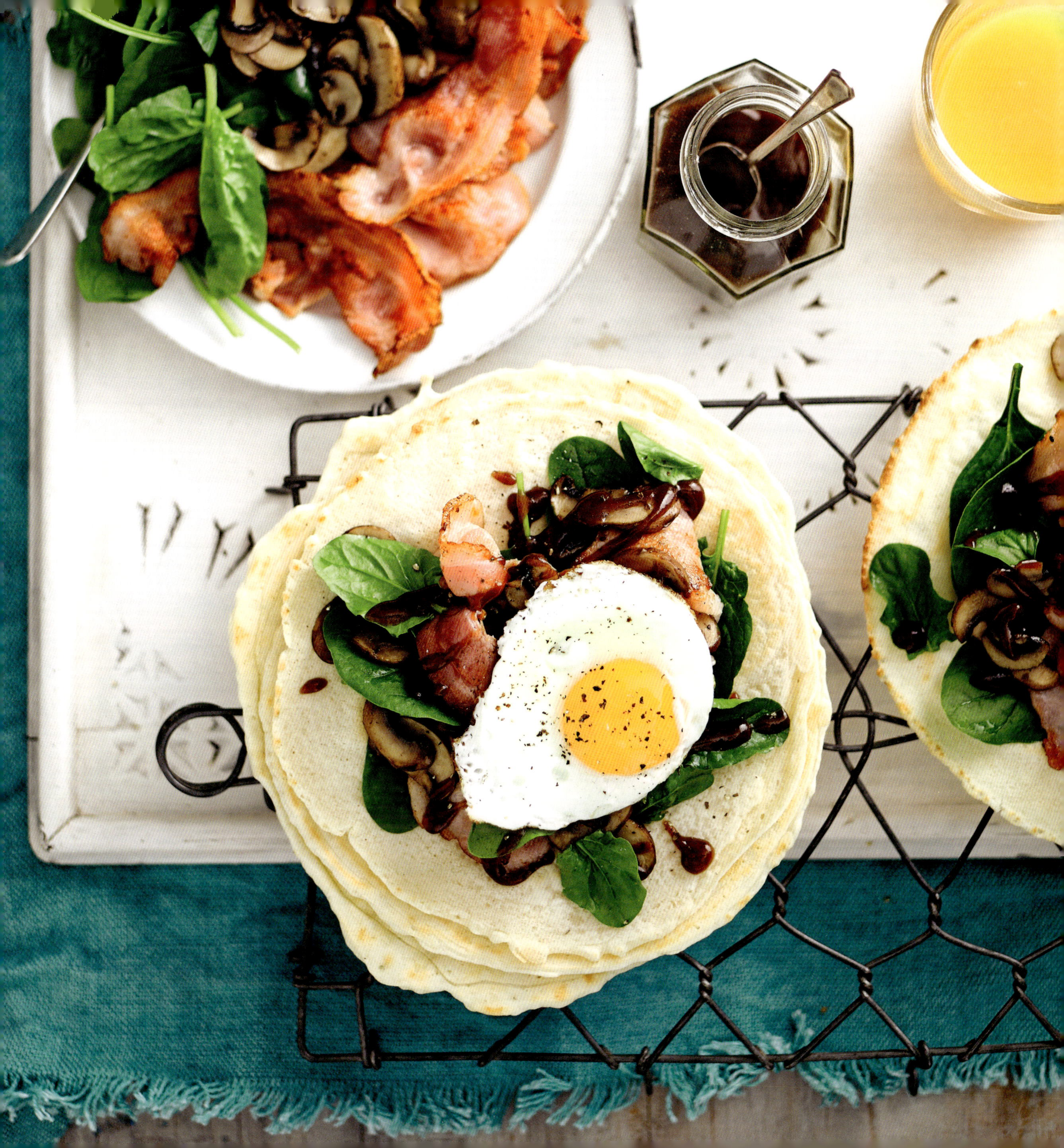

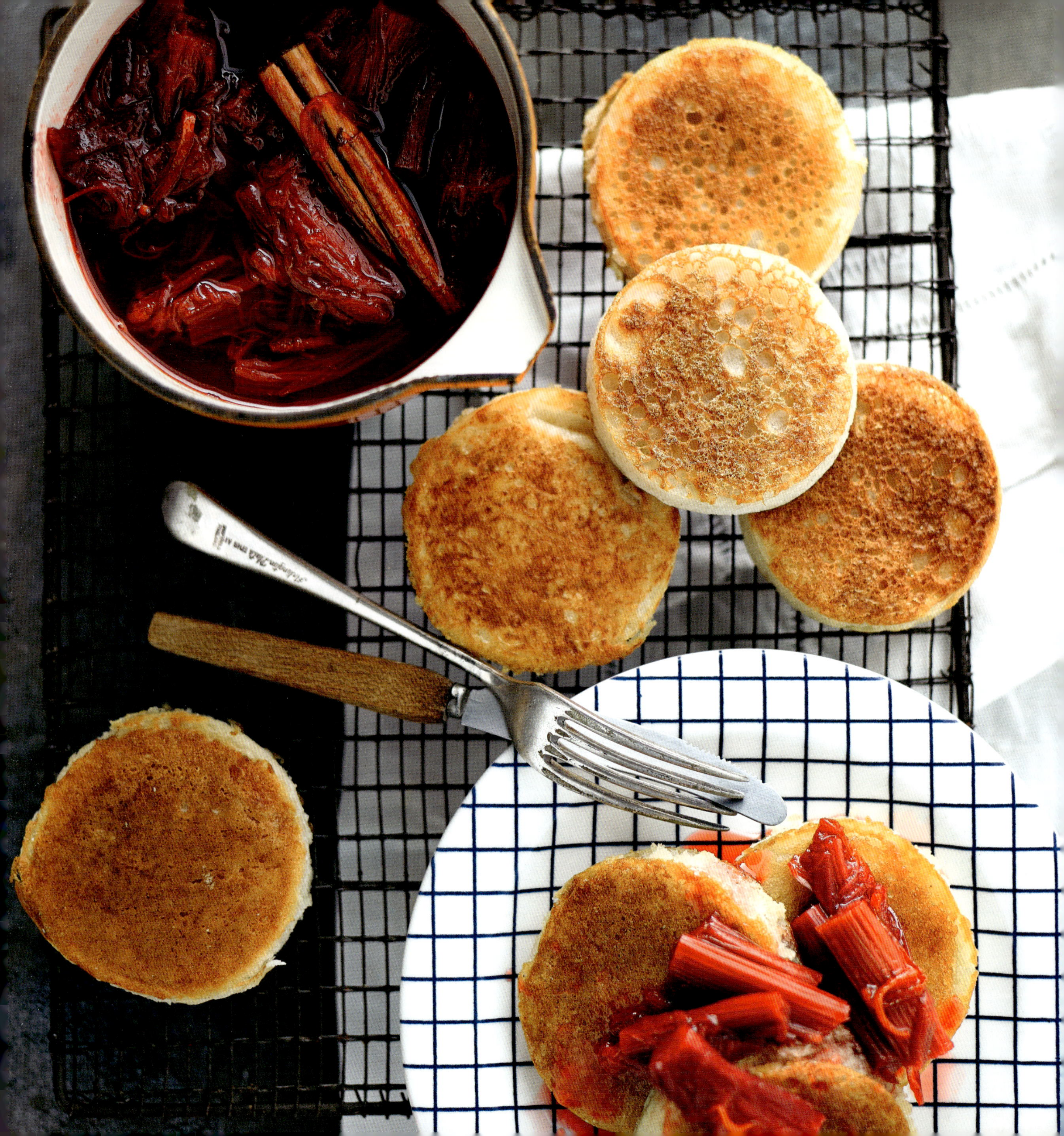

BREAKFAST

GLUTEN FREE • DAIRY FREE • EGG FREE • NUT FREE

CRUMPETS WITH RHUBARB COMPOTE

PREP + COOK TIME 1 HOUR (+ STANDING) SERVES 8

You need 4 egg rings for this recipe.

1½ cups (375ml) warm water

2 teaspoons (7g) dry yeast

1½ cups (200g) gluten-free plain (all-purpose) flour

½ cup (75g) 100% corn (maize) cornflour (cornstarch)

1½ teaspoons salt

2 tablespoons brown sugar

¼ cup (60ml) soy milk

1 tablespoon dairy-free spread

RHUBARB COMPOTE

300g (9½ ounces) trimmed rhubarb, cut into 4cm (1½-inch) lengths

1 cinnamon stick

1 tablespoon finely grated orange rind

⅓ cup (80ml) orange juice

¼ cup (55g) caster (superfine) sugar

1 Combine ¼ cup of the water and all the yeast in a small bowl. Cover; stand in a warm place for 10 minutes or until mixture is frothy.
2 Sift flours into a medium bowl; stir in salt and sugar. Make a well in the centre; gradually whisk in the milk and the remaining water until combined. Add the yeast mixture; whisk until smooth. Cover; stand in a warm place for 30 minutes or until mixture has risen slightly.
3 Melt dairy-free spread.
4 Heat a large heavy-based frying pan over low heat. Brush a little of the melted spread over base of pan and around the insides of four egg rings; place rings in pan.
5 Pour 2 tablespoons of batter into each ring; cook, uncovered, until bubbles appear and the surface is a little dry. Using egg slide, turn rings; cook for 1 minute or until crumpets are cooked through. Remove from pan; cover to keep warm. Repeat to make 16 crumpets in total, brushing pan and rings with melted spread between each batch.
6 Meanwhile, make rhubarb compote.
7 Serve crumpets topped with compote.

RHUBARB COMPOTE Combine ingredients in a medium suacepan over medium heat; simmer, covered, for 5 minutes or until rhubarb is tender.

nutritional count per serving 1.9g total fat (0.4g saturated fat); 807kJ (193 cal); 41g carbohydrate; 2.1g protein; 1g fibre

tips You can use your favourite dairy-free milk for this recipe or, if you don't have a dairy allergy, use whichever milk you like. Crumpets are best made just before serving.

GLUTEN FREE · DAIRY FREE · NUT FREE

GRANOLA WITH PLUMS

PREP + COOK TIME 40 MINUTES (+ COOLING) **SERVES** 4

Preheat oven to 150°C/300°F. Line a large oven tray with baking paper. Combine 1 cup each of gluten-free cornflakes, rice-bran cereal and puffed rice and ⅓ cup pepitas and sunflower seed mix in a large bowl. Drizzle with ¼ cup honey and 1 tablespoon vegetable oil; sprinkle with ½ teaspoon ground cinnamon. Toss gently to combine. Spread evenly on an oven tray. Bake, turning occasionally, for 20 minutes or until lightly golden. Stir through ½ cup thickly sliced dried figs and ⅓ cup sultanas; cool granola. Divide granola into serving bowls; drizzle evenly with 700g vanilla soy yoghurt and top each bowl with 2 plums in natural syrup.

nutritional count per serving 5.8g total fat (1.9g saturated fat); 2550kJ (609 cal); 99g carbohydrate; 13.9g protein; 10.9g fibre

USE YOUR FAVOURITE DRIED FRUIT INSTEAD OF FIGS AND SULTANAS, AND YOUR FAVOURITE VANILLA YOGHURT, IF YOU DON'T HAVE A DAIRY ALLERGY.

GLUTEN FREE · DAIRY FREE · NUT FREE

HONEY BAKED MUESLI

PREP + COOK TIME 1 HOUR (+ COOLING) SERVES 4

Preheat oven to 180°C/350°F. Grease and line a large baking tray. Combine 1 cup rice flakes, 1½ cups gluten-free corn flakes and 1½ cups puffed rice in tray. Combine ⅓ cup honey, 2 tablespoons water and 1 cinnamon stick in a small saucepan; bring to the boil, reduce heat, simmer for 5 minutes or until thickened slightly. Discard cinnamon stick. Pour honey mixture over cereal in baking tray; toss to coat. Bake, uncovered, 40 minutes or until browned lightly, stirring twice during cooking time. Cool; stir in 1½ cups nut-free trail mix. To serve, divide muesli into bowls; evenly top with 1 cup coconut milk yoghurt and ⅓ cup passionfruit pulp.

nutritional count per serving 11.2g total fat (4.2g saturated fat); 2194kJ (524 cal); 83.4g carbohydrate; 17.1g protein; 3g fibre

tips Store muesli in an airtight container in the fridge for up to 3 months. Serve with your favourite yoghurt or milk, if you don't have a dairy allergy.

BREAKFAST

GLUTEN FREE • DAIRY FREE • EGG FREE • NUT FREE

SAUSAGE, MUSHROOM AND ROASTED TOMATO ROLLS

PREP + COOK TIME 40 MINUTES   SERVES 4

4 small roma (egg) tomatoes (240g), halved

400g (12½ ounces) button or cup mushrooms, sliced thickly

1 clove garlic, chopped finely

1 tablespoon olive oil

2 teaspoons balsamic vinegar

cooking-oil spray

8 gluten-free beef chipolata sausages (400g)

80g (2½ ounces) baby spinach leaves

4 gluten-free, wheat-free, egg-free bread rolls (200g), split, toasted

1 Preheat oven to 150°C/300°F.
2 Combine tomato, mushrooms and garlic in a medium roasting pan, drizzle with oil and vinegar; toss to coat, season. Bake for 30 minutes or until tomatoes begin to soften. Cool slightly.
3 Spray a large frying pan with oil; heat over medium heat. Cook sausages until golden brown and cooked through. Cool slightly; slice thickly lengthways.
4 To serve, sandwich spinach, tomato, mushrooms and sausage between bread roll halves.

nutritional count per serving 34.9g total fat (14.3g saturated fat); 2398kJ (573 cal); 36.7g carbohydrate; 25.4g protein; 6.8g fibre

tips Check the sausages that you buy are gluten-free as some sausages contain gluten. You can make the gluten-free bread recipe on page 58 into bread rolls

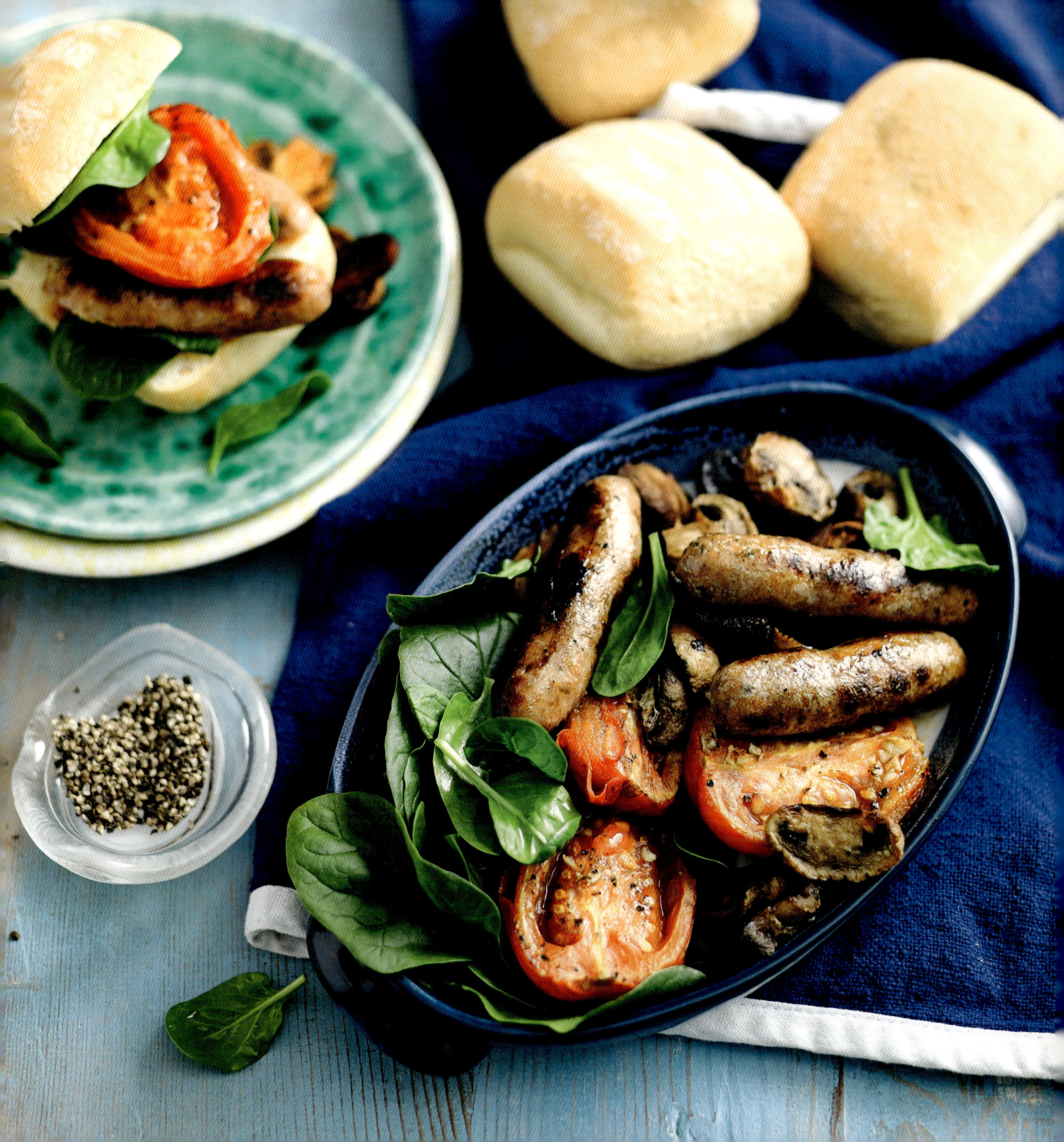

IF YOU ARE PRESSED FOR TIME, MAKE ONE BIG OMELETTE IN A MEDIUM FRYING PAN. YOU CAN CHANGE THE FILLING DEPENDING ON THE SEASONAL VEGETABLES AVAILABLE – TRY ADDING PUMPKIN OR BROCCOLINI.

BREAKFAST

GLUTEN FREE • DAIRY FREE • NUT FREE

OMELETTE WITH ASPARAGUS AND MINT

PREP + COOK TIME 20 MINUTES SERVES 4

2 baby new potatoes (80g), cut into 5mm (¼-inch) cubes

340g (11 ounces) asparagus, trimmed

2 cup (240g) frozen peas

4 eggs

½ cup coarsely chopped fresh mint leaves

2 tablespoon olive oil

2 slices gluten-free bread (90g), toasted

1 Cook potato in a small saucepan of boiling water for 3 minutes. Add asparagus and peas; cook a further 1 minute or until asparagus is bright green and potato is tender. Drain. When cool enough to handle, cut the asparagus in half; finely chop the stem ends.
2 Lightly whisk eggs in a medium bowl; stir in potato, peas, mint and chopped asparagus ends.
3 Heat 2 teaspoons of the oil in a small non-stick frying pan on high; cook a quarter of the egg mixture, for about 2 minutes, pulling in the egg with a spatula to help it cook quickly. Fold over; slide onto a warm serving plate. Repeat with remaining oil and egg mixture to make a total of four omelettes.
4 Serve omelettes with remaining asparagus and toast.

nutritional count per serving 15.8g total fat (3.4g saturated fat); 1400kJ (335 cal); 27.7g carbohydrate; 16.3g protein; 8.8g fibre

BREAKFAST

GLUTEN FREE • DAIRY FREE • EGG FREE • YEAST FREE • NUT FREE

RASPBERRY AND BANANA BREAD

PREP + COOK TIME 1¾ HOURS (+ COOLING) SERVES 8

You need 3 large overripe bananas (690g) for the mashed banana in this recipe.

1½ cups (350g) mashed banana

½ cup (125ml) vegetable oil

½ cup (125ml) soy milk

2½ cups (335g) gluten-free self-raising flour

1¼ cups (275g) firmly packed brown sugar

½ teaspoon bicarbonate of soda (baking soda)

1 cup (80g) desiccated coconut

1 cup (150g) frozen raspberries

20g (¾ ounce) dairy-free spread

1 large banana (230g), sliced thickly diagonally

⅓ cup (100g) golden syrup

1 Preheat oven to 180°C/375°F. Grease a 10cm x 20cm (4-inch x 8-inch) loaf pan; line base and long sides with baking paper, extending the paper 5cm (2 inches) over the sides.
2 Combine mashed banana, oil and milk in a small bowl.
3 Combine sifted flour, sugar and bicarbonate of soda with coconut in a large bowl. Make a well in the centre. Pour banana mixture into well; stir to combine. Fold in raspberries until just combined. Spoon mixture into pan; smooth the surface.
4 Bake bread about 1¼ hours or until a skewer inserted into the centre comes out clean. Stand bread in pan for 5 minutes before turning, top-side up, onto a wire rack to cool.
5 Melt dairy-free spread in a large frying pan over high heat, add sliced banana; cook 1 minute each side or until caramelised. Thickly slice bread, top with banana; drizzle with golden syrup.

nutritional count per serving 23g total fat (7.4g saturated fat); 2464kJ (588 cal); 93.4g carbohydrate; 2.7g protein; 4.3g fibre

USE YOUR FAVOURITE DAIRY-FREE MILK FOR THIS RECIPE. YOU CAN REPLACE THE RASPBERRIES WITH BLUEBERRIES OR CHOPPED PEAR, OR LEAVE THE FRUIT OUT ALTOGETHER. CUT THE BREAD INTO PORTION-SIZED PIECES AND FREEZE IN AN AIRTIGHT CONTAINER FOR UP TO 3 MONTHS. THE BREAD CAN BE TOASTED TO SERVE.

GLUTEN FREE • DAIRY FREE • NUT FREE

MAPLE GLAZED PUFFED CORN

PREP + COOK TIME 30 MINUTES (+ COOLING) **SERVES** 4

Preheat oven to 180°C/350°F. Grease and line a large baking tray with baking paper. Combine 6 cups puffed corn and 1 cup maple syrup on tray; toss to coat. Bake, uncovered, stirring occasionally, for 20 minutes or until golden brown. Cool on tray. Serve with ½ cup vanilla soy yoghurt.

nutritional count per serving 0.6g total fat (0g saturated fat); 1379kJ (329 cal); 79.5g carbohydrate; 3.1g protein; 0.2g fibre

STORE IN AN AIRTIGHT CONTAINER IN THE FRIDGE FOR UP TO 3 MONTHS. SERVE IN LITTLE NOODLE BOXES OR PAPER CONES AS AN AFTERNOON SNACK, IF YOU LIKE.

GLUTEN FREE · DAIRY FREE · NUT FREE

BIRCHER MUESLI

PREP TIME 15 MINUTES (+ REFRIGERATION) **SERVES** 4

Combine 2 cups gluten-free quick oats, 1 large coarsely grated green apple, ½ cup apple juice, ⅓ cup orange juice, ½ cup vanilla soy yoghurt, 1 tablespoon caster (superfine) sugar, 1 tablespoon finely grated orange rind, ½ teaspoon ground cinnamon and ¼ teaspoon ground cardamom in a large bowl. Cover with plastic wrap; refrigerate for 1 hour or overnight. Add 125g (4 ounces) blueberries; stir to combine. Top with extra orange rind to serve, if you like.

nutritional count per serving 2.1g total fat (0.3g saturated fat); 747kJ (193 cal); 34.3g carbohydrate; 3.9g protein; 3.9g fibre

tip Use Greek-style yoghurt if you don't have a dairy allergy.

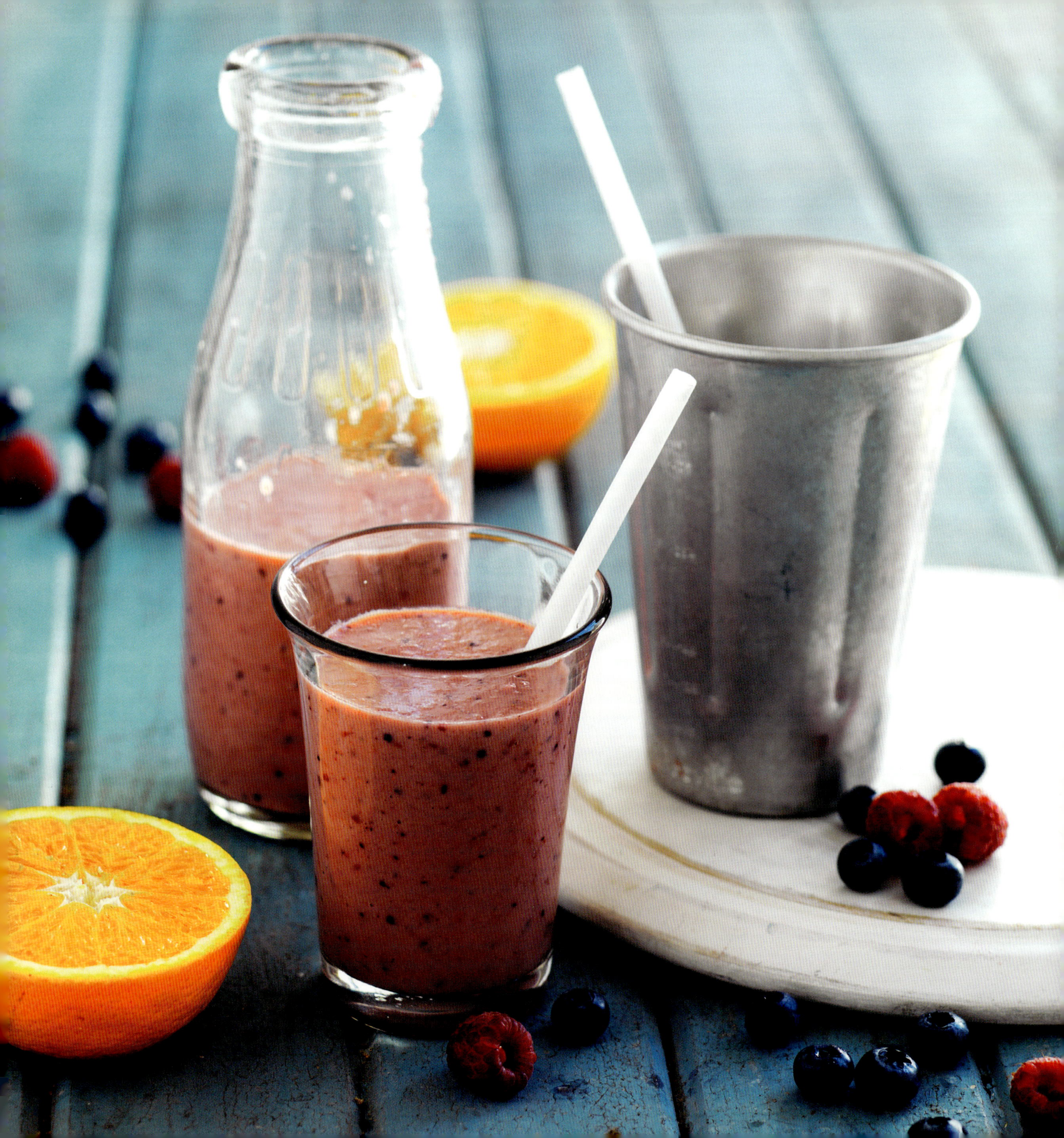

BREAKFAST

GLUTEN FREE • EGG FREE • NUT FREE

ORANGE BERRY SMOOTHIE

PREP TIME 10 MINUTES SERVES 4

2 medium oranges (440g), peeled, chopped roughly
2 medium pears (460g), cored, chopped roughly
2 cups (300g) frozen mixed berries
150g (4½ ounces) low-fat gluten-free vanilla yoghurt
¼ cup (60ml) pomegranate juice

1 Blend or process orange and pear until well combined.
2 Add berries, yoghurt and juice; blend until smooth.

nutritional count per serving 0.4g total fat (0.1g saturated fat); 862kJ (206 cal); 38.9g carbohydrate; 6.4g protein; 9.4g fibre

tip You could use apple juice instead of the pomegranate juice, if you prefer. You can use your favourite berries in this recipe.

LUNCH

BEFORE YOU START BASIC STEPS

TRIMMING SNOW PEAS
Use a sharp knife to trim the ends from the snow pea, then pull to remove the thin string from one side of the pea. Remove the string from the other side. Use whole, or slice the snow peas thinly as directed by the recipe.

SHREDDING WOMBOK
Use a V-slicer or mandoline to quickly and easily shred wombok. Slide the wombok back and forth across the blade. The adjustable blade is very sharp, so watch your fingers and use the guard supplied.

LUNCH

TRIMMING BEETROOT
Cut the stems to 2cm (¾ inch) of the bulb. Don't trim the beard at the base of the root, as this stops the colour from bleeding during cooking. The beetroot leaves can be added to salads.

ROLLING OUT PASTRY
Roll the pastry between sheets of baking paper, from the centre, without rolling over the edge. Roll from the centre up, then the centre down; give a quarter turn then repeat. This keeps the pastry even and in a rounded shape.

LUNCH

GLUTEN FREE • DAIRY FREE • EGG FREE • NUT FREE

SALMON AND QUINOA SALAD

PREP + COOK TIME 25 MINUTES SERVES 4

1 cup (200g) quinoa
3 cups (750ml) water
200g (6½ ounces) snow peas, trimmed, sliced thinly lengthways
1 lebanese cucumber (130g), halved lengthways, sliced thinly crossways
½ cup small fresh mint leaves
¼ cup (60ml) lemon juice
2 tablespoons olive oil
150g (4½ ounces) hot-smoked salmon, skinned, flaked coarsely
1 tablespoon thinly sliced lemon rind (see tips)

1 Combine quinoa and the water in a large saucepan; bring to the boil. Reduce heat to low; cook, covered, for 15 minutes or until liquid is absorbed and quinoa is tender. Rinse, drain well.

2 Place snow peas in a heatproof bowl. Cover with boiling water; stand for 2 minutes. Refresh under cold running water; drain well.

3 Place quinoa and snow peas in a large bowl with cucumber and mint; toss to combine. Season to taste. Add combined juice and oil; toss to coat. Serve salad topped with salmon and rind.

nutritional count per serving 16.2g total fat (2.6g saturated fat); 1556kJ (372 cal); 35g carbohydrate; 19.3g protein; 5.1g fibre

tips Use a zesting tool for the lemon rind. You can use freshly cooked salmon, coarsely flaked smoked trout or smoked chicken for an alternative. Add asparagus and snow pea sprouts for extra crunch.

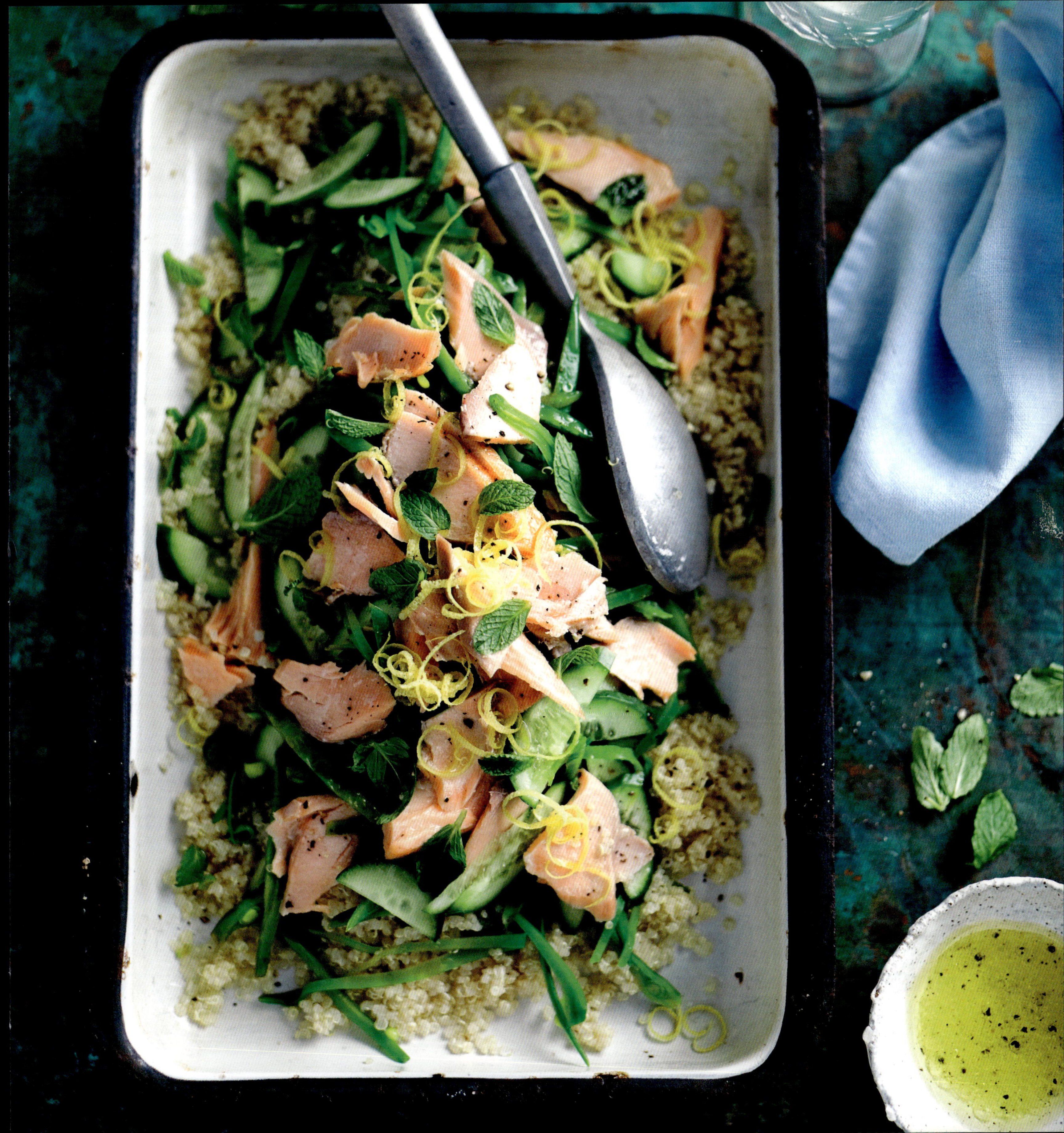

LUNCH

GLUTEN FREE • DAIRY FREE • EGG FREE • NUT FREE

COCONUT CHICKEN AND RICE NOODLE SALAD

PREP + COOK TIME 30 MINUTES (+ COOLING & REFRIGERATION) SERVES 4

2 chicken breast fillets (400g)

4 kaffir lime leaves

400ml (12½ ounces) canned coconut milk

200g (6½ ounces) dried rice stick noodles

½ small wombok (napa cabbage) (350g), shredded finely

1 large carrot (180g), cut into matchsticks

1 cup (80g) bean sprouts

½ cup loosely packed fresh mint leaves

½ cup loosely packed fresh coriander (cilantro) leaves

¼ cup (60ml) lime juice

2 tablespoons brown sugar

2 tablespoons fish sauce

1 Place chicken and 2 of the lime leaves in a medium saucepan. Add coconut milk and enough cold water to cover the chicken. Bring to a simmer over high heat then reduce heat to low; simmer, uncovered, 10 minutes or until the chicken is cooked through. Cool completely.
2 Remove chicken from pan; reserve ¼ cup of the cooking liquid (discard remainder). Coarsely shred the chicken meat into a large bowl; add reserved cooking liquid. Cover with plastic wrap; refrigerate until cold.
3 Place dried noodles in a large heatproof bowl; cover with boiling water. Stand until just tender; drain. Rinse under cold water; drain well.
4 Add noodles, wombok, carrot and sprouts to chicken mixture; toss to combine. Finely shred remaining lime leaves; add to noodle mixture with mint and coriander.
5 Place juice, sugar and sauce in a screw-top jar; shake until combined. Pour dressing over salad; toss gently to combine. Serve salad with lime wedges, if you like.

nutritional count per serving 4.2g total fat (2.4g saturated fat); 1009kJ (241 cal); 20g carbohydrate; 27.7g protein; 5.3g fibre

USE ANY STYLE OF RICE NOODLE YOU LIKE. THE RECIPE CAN BE MADE A DAY AHEAD; STORE, COVERED, IN THE FRIDGE. KEEP THE DRESSING SEPARATE AND DRESS JUST BEFORE SERVING. THIS IS A GREAT RECIPE FOR LUNCH AT THE OFFICE OR FOR A PICNIC.

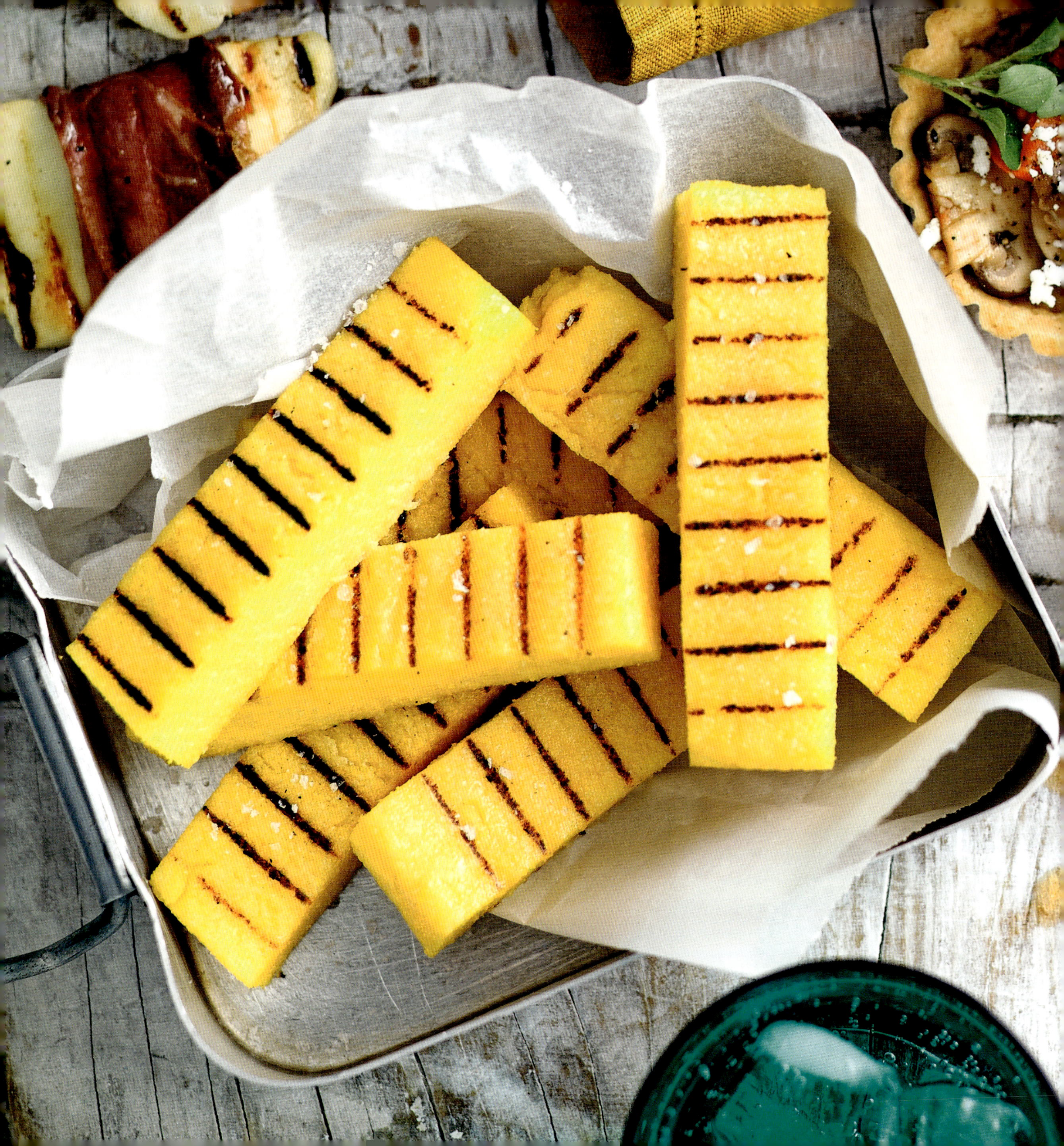

LUNCH

GLUTEN FREE • EGG FREE • NUT FREE
CHEESY POLENTA FINGERS

PREP + COOK TIME 25 MINUTES (+ REFRIGERATION) **MAKES** 16

Serve these cheesy polenta fingers on a mezze-style platter with prosciutto-wrapped haloumi, mixed olives and baby gherkins, and individual mushroom and tomato tarts.

2½ cups (625ml) chicken stock

1 cup (170g) polenta

½ cup (40g) finely grated parmesan

¼ cup (25g) pizza cheese

1 tablespoon olive oil

1 Grease a deep 19cm (8-inch) square cake pan; line base and sides with baking paper.
2 Boil stock in a medium saucepan; gradually stir in polenta. Simmer, stirring, for 10 minutes or until thickened. Stir in cheeses. Spread mixture into pan; smooth surface with the back of a spoon. Cover; refrigerate 1 hour or until firm.
3 Turn polenta onto a clean surface; cut into 16 fingers, about 1.5cm x 9.5cm (⅜-inch x 4-inch) in size.
4 Brush polenta with oil; cook on a heated oiled grill pan (or grill or barbecue) for 3 minutes each side or until browned lightly and heated through.

nutritional count per finger 2.7g total fat (1g saturated fat); 148kJ (35 cal); 7.6g carbohydrate; 2.5g protein; 0.3g fibre

tips Polenta can be prepared 2 days ahead; store, covered, in the fridge. The fingers can be eaten cold or warm, and are great in lunchboxes for a healthy snack. Fresh chopped herbs can be stirred through the polenta, if you like.

LUNCH

GLUTEN FREE • NUT FREE
MUSHROOM AND TOMATO TARTS

PREP + COOK TIME 25 MINUTES (+ REFRIGERATION) MAKES 12

You will need an 8cm (3¼-inch) round cutter.

½ quantity gluten-free pastry (see page 105)

1 teaspoon butter

120g (4 ounces) swiss brown mushrooms, sliced thinly

1 tablespoon red wine vinegar

12 cherry tomatoes, quartered

60g (2 ounces) fetta, crumbled

1 tablespoon fresh oregano leaves

1 Grease 12 x 6cm (2½-inch) tart tins. Roll pastry between sheets of baking paper until 3mm (⅛-inch) thick; cut 12 rounds from pastry using cutter. Ease pastry into tins, pressing into base and side; trim edges, prick base with a fork. Place tart tins on an oven tray; cover, refrigerate for 30 minutes.
2 Preheat oven to 180°C/350°F.
3 Bake pastry cases for 10 minutes or until browned lightly. Cool.
4 Melt butter in a small frying pan over high heat, add mushrooms; cook until softened. Add vinegar; cook, stirring, until liquid is reduced. Add tomatoes; cook, stirring, until heated through. Remove from heat; season to taste. Cool 10 minutes.
5 Spoon mushroom mixture into tart cases; sprinkle with fetta and oregano just before serving.

nutritional count per tart 7.5g total fat (4g saturated fat); 541kJ (129 cal); 13.1g carbohydrate; 1.9g protein; 0.7g fibre

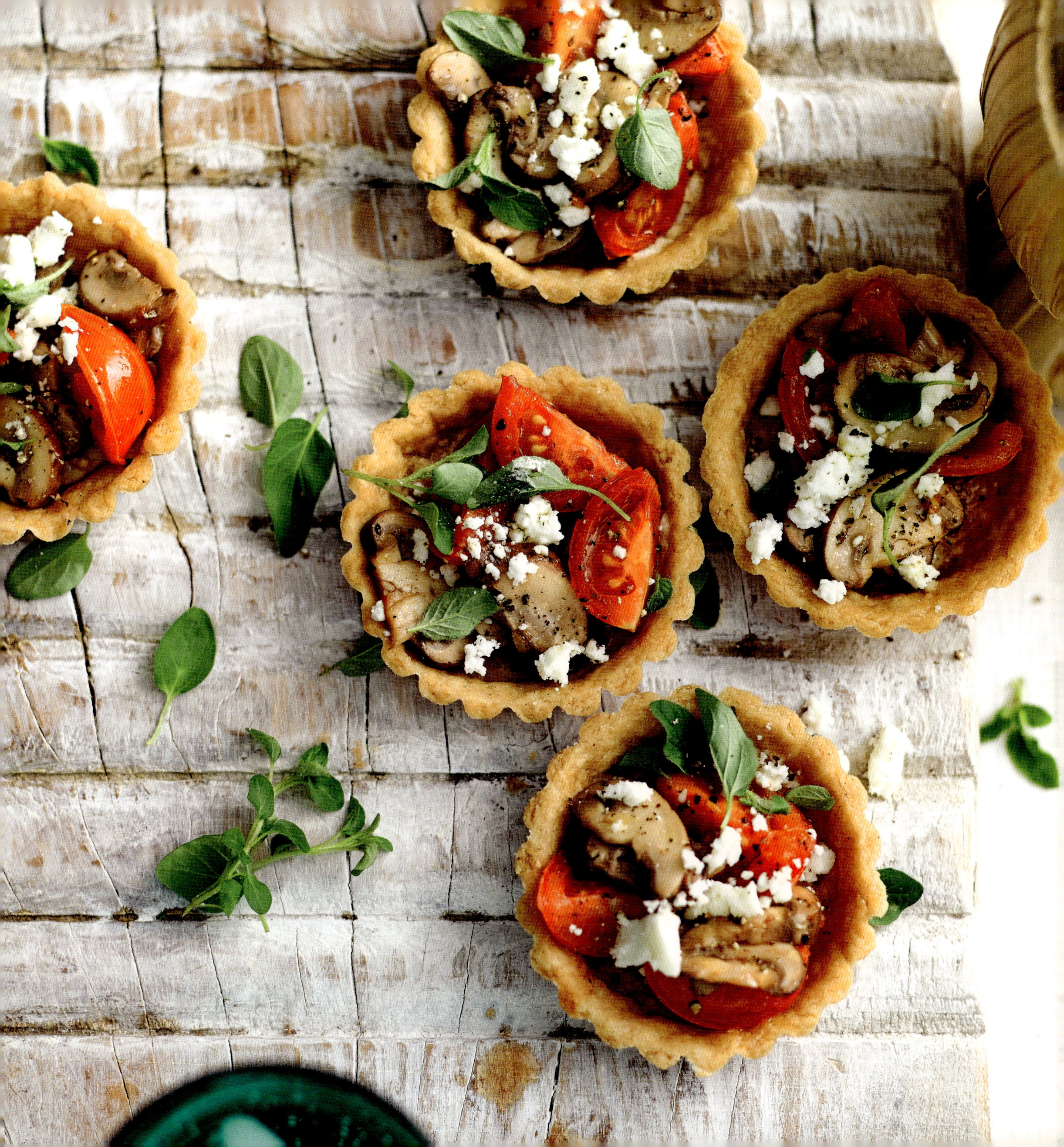

ADD A COOKED KING PRAWN TO THE HALOUMI, AND WRAP THEM BOTH IN THE PROSCIUTTO BEFORE COOKING.

LUNCH

GLUTEN FREE • NUT FREE

PROSCIUTTO-WRAPPED HALOUMI

PREP + COOK TIME 25 MINUTES MAKES 12

250g (8 ounces) haloumi cheese

6 slices gluten-free prosciutto (90g)

1 tablespoon lemon juice

1 clove garlic, crushed

450g (14½ ounces) bottled mixed olives and baby gherkins, drained

1 Cut haloumi into 12 slices. Cut prosciutto in half crossways; wrap haloumi in prosciutto.
2 Cook haloumi on a heated oiled grill pan (or grill or barbecue) over medium heat, 2 minutes each side or until prosciutto starts to crisp.
3 Drizzle with combined juice and garlic; season to taste. Serve with mixed olives and gherkins.

nutritional count per piece 9.1g total fat (3.4g saturated fat); 490kJ (117 cal); 1.1g carbohydrate; 6.9g protein; 0.1g fibre

LUNCH

GLUTEN FREE • DAIRY FREE • NUT FREE

GLUTEN-FREE BREAD

PREP + COOK TIME 1½ HOURS (+ STANDING) MAKES 1 LOAF (12 SLICES)

3 cups (405g) gluten-free plain (all-purpose) flour
½ cup (75g) potato flour
½ cup (80g) brown rice flour
½ cup (80g) white rice flour
3 teaspoons (10g) dried yeast
2 teaspoons salt
2 teaspoons xantham gum
1 egg
3 egg whites
¾ cup (180ml) olive oil
1 teaspoon vinegar
2 cups (500ml) warm water
1 tablespoon olive oil, extra
2 teaspoons salt, extra

1 Grease a 12cm x 20cm (4¾-inch x 8-inch) loaf pan; lightly dust with rice flour.
2 Combine sifted flours, yeast, salt and gum in a large bowl.
3 Place egg, egg whites, oil, vinegar and 1½ cups of the water in a large bowl of an electric mixer; beat on medium speed for 3½ minutes. Add remaining water and the flour mixture, 1 cup at a time, beating until combined and smooth.
4 Spoon mixture into loaf pan; smooth the surface. Cover; stand in a warm place for 45 minutes.
5 Preheat oven to 220°C/425°F.
6 Drizzle loaf with extra oil and sprinkle with extra salt. Bake for 1 hour or until crust is firm and golden brown and the loaf sounds hollow when tapped. Stand bread in pan for 5 minutes before turning, top-side up, onto a wire rack to cool.

nutritional count per slice 16.1g total fat (2.4g saturated fat); 1400kJ (335 cal); 43.8g carbohydrate; 3g protein; 0.7g fibre

This bread is best eaten the day it is baked, however, it's great for toast or toasted sandwiches the next day. This mixture will make 6 gluten-free bread rolls – divide dough into 6 even portions, roll into balls and place on a greased and floured baking tray, stand 45 minutes. Drizzle rolls with oil and sprinkle with salt; bake for 30 minutes.

GLUTEN FREE · DAIRY FREE · NUT FREE

PASTRAMI WITH SILVER BEET COLESLAW

PREP TIME 20 MINUTES   SERVES 2

Combine 2 medium finely shredded silver beet leaves, 1 medium carrot, cut into matchsticks, 1 thinly sliced green onion (scallion), 2 tablespoons plain soy yoghurt and 1½ teaspoons dijon mustard in a medium bowl. Season to taste. Sandwich 100g (3 ounces) pastrami slices and silver beet mixture between four slices of gluten-free bread.

nutritional count per serving 3.9g total fat (1g saturated fat); 883kJ (211 cal); 27.3g carbohydrate; 14.3g protein; 4.3g fibre

tips Use your favourite brand of gluten-free bread or make the recipe on page 58. If you like, replace the mustard with gluten-free horseradish and use roast beef slices instead of the pastrami.

USE YOUR FAVOURITE BRAND OF GLUTEN-FREE BREAD OR MAKE THE RECIPE ON PAGE 58. YOU CAN USE POACHED CHICKEN BREAST OR SALMON INSTEAD OF TUNA.

GLUTEN FREE • DAIRY FREE • NUT FREE

TUNA WITH QUINOA TABBOULEH

PREP + COOK TIME **25 MINUTES (+ COOLING)** SERVES **2**

Bring ¼ cup rinsed, drained quinoa and ¾ cup of water to the boil in a small saucepan over high heat. Reduce heat to low; cook, covered, for 15 minutes or until liquid is absorbed. Cool. Transfer quinoa to a small bowl; add 1 finely chopped medium tomato, 1 finely sliced green onion (scallion), 2 tablespoons each of coarsely chopped fresh flat-leaf parsley and mint, 1 tablespoon olive oil and 1½ tablespoons lemon juice; toss to combine. Fold 95g (3 ounces) canned drained flaked tuna in oil through salad. Season to taste. Sandwich salad between two small halved gluten-free turkish bread rolls.

nutritional count per serving 19.3g total fat (2.9g saturated fat); 1764kJ (421 cal); 40.7g carbohydrate; 19.3g protein; 4.7g fibre

LUNCH

GLUTEN FREE • NUT FREE

OLIVE AND BACON PIZZA SCROLLS

PREP + COOK TIME 50 MINUTES MAKES 12

⅓ quantity basic gluten-free pizza dough (see page 117)

potato flour, for dusting

1½ tablespoons tomato paste

3 rindless gluten-free bacon slices (195g), chopped coarsely

¼ cup (40g) sliced black olives

1 tablespoon coarsely chopped fresh oregano

1 cup (100g) grated mozzarella

1 Preheat oven to 220°C/425°F. Oil a 19cm x 29cm (8-inch x 11¾-inch) rectangular pan.
2 Turn pizza dough onto a work surface dusted with potato flour. Roll dough into a 25cm x 30cm (10-inch x 12-inch) rectangle.
3 Spread tomato paste over dough, leaving a 1cm (½-inch) border; sprinkle dough with bacon, olives, oregano and ½ cup of the cheese. Firmly roll dough from long side to enclose filling; trim ends.
4 Cut roll into 12 slices; place slices, cut-side up, in a single layer, in pan.
5 Bake scrolls for 20 minutes; top with remaining cheese. Bake a further 15 minutes or until cheese has melted and turns golden brown. Sprinkle with oregano leaves to serve, if you like.

nutritional count per scroll 9.6g total fat (2.8g saturated fat); 801kJ (241 cal); 19.4g carbohydrate; 6.5g protein; 0.5g fibre

tips Serve scrolls warm or cold. This is a great recipe for kids' lunchboxes. You can leave out the olives and oregano if your child doesn't like those flavours, and just make them using bacon and cheese. Store scrolls in an airtight container for 1 day, or freeze, wrapped in plastic wrap, for up to 3 months. To reheat: discard plastic, and wrap frozen scrolls in foil; place in a moderate oven for 30 minutes or until heated through.

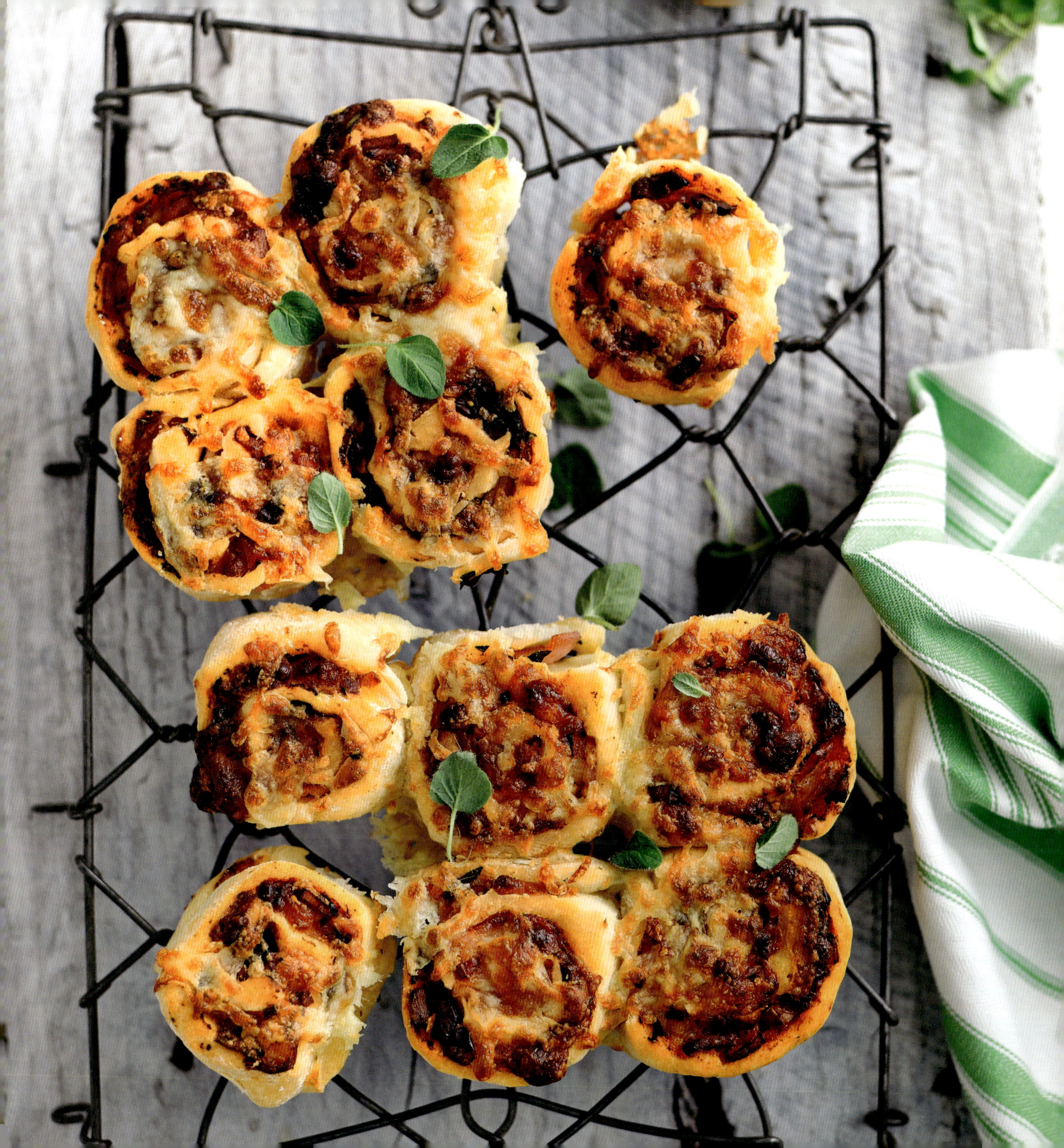

Rice balls can be made 3 days ahead; store, covered, in the refrigerator. The tomato chutney can be made 1 week ahead; store in a sterilised jar (see page 186), in the fridge. Swap the mozzarella filling for anchovies or olives, if you like.

LUNCH

GLUTEN FREE • NUT FREE

CHEESY RICE BALLS WITH TOMATO CHUTNEY

PREP + COOK TIME 50 MINUTES (+ REFRIGERATION)   SERVES 4

⅔ cup (130g) white short-grain rice

1⅓ cups (330ml) water

150g (4½ ounces) mozzarella

3 eggs

½ cup (40g) finely grated parmesan

100g (3 ounces) fetta, crumbled

⅔ cup (100g) 100% corn (maize) cornflour (cornstarch)

3 cups (300g) gluten-free breadcrumbs

vegetable oil, for deep frying

TOMATO CHUTNEY

2 large tomatoes (440g), chopped coarsely

1 medium red onion (170g), chopped coarsely

1½ tablespoons red wine vinegar

2 cloves garlic, chopped coarsely

1 tablespoon brown sugar

1 Combine rice and the water in a medium heavy-based saucepan. Cover tightly, bring to the boil; reduce heat to as low as possible, cook for 10 minutes. Remove pan from heat; stand, covered, for 5 minutes.

2 Cut mozzarella into 28 x 5mm (¼-inch) cubes.

3 Combine rice, 1 egg, parmesan and fetta in a medium bowl. Roll rounded tablespoons of rice mixture into 28 balls; press a piece of mozzarella into the centre of each ball, roll to enclose.

4 Lightly beat remaining eggs. Coat balls in cornflour; dip in egg, then coat in breadcrumbs. Cover balls; refrigerate for 30 minutes.

5 Meanwhile, make tomato chutney.

6 Heat oil in a large heavy-based saucepan over medium-high heat until oil reaches 190°C/375°F on a sugar thermometer (or when a cube of bread turns golden in about 10 seconds). Deep-fry balls, in batches, for 4 minutes or until golden and heated through; drain on paper towel.

7 Serve rice balls warm or cold with tomato chutney; sprinkle with fresh parsley leaves, if you like.

TOMATO CHUTNEY Place ingredients in a medium saucepan over medium-high heat; cook, uncovered, stirring occasionally, for 10 minutes or until mixture is soft. Blend or process mixture until just combined.

nutritional count per serving 37.2g total fat (14.5g saturated fat); 3325kJ (794 cal); 104.8g carbohydrate; 30.8g protein; 2.7g fibre

LUNCH

GLUTEN FREE • DAIRY FREE • EGG FREE • YEAST FREE • NUT FREE

BEETROOT HUMMUS AND BEEF WRAP

PREP + COOK TIME 1¼ HOURS MAKES 4

4 baby beetroot (100g), unpeeled, trimmed
1 small zucchini (90g), sliced thinly lengthways
420g (13½ ounces) canned chickpeas, drained, rinsed
1 tablespoon tahini
1 clove garlic, crushed
1 tablespoon lemon juice
⅓ cup (80ml) olive oil
4 gluten-free wraps (260g) (see tips)
320g (10 ounces) rare roast beef
80g (2½ ounces) baby rocket (arugula) leaves

1 Preheat oven to 180°C/350°F.
2 Wrap each beetroot in a piece of foil; place in a small shallow baking dish. Roast 50 minutes or until tender. When cool enough to handle, peel beetroot then cut into quarters.
3 Meanwhile, cook zucchini on a heated, oiled, grill pan (or grill or barbecue) for 3 minutes each side or until browned and tender.
4 Blend or process beetroot, chickpeas, tahini, garlic and juice until combined. With motor operating, gradually add oil in a thin steady stream; process until mixture is smooth. Season to taste.
5 Spread wraps with beetroot hummus; top with beef, rocket and zucchini, roll to enclose filling.

nutritional count per wrap 29g total fat (4.8g saturated fat); 2486kJ (549 cal); 56.9g carbohydrate; 23.7g protein; 5.5g fibre

tips Use your favourite wrap, or make the gluten-free wraps from the breakfast wraps recipe on page 28. Beetroot hummus can be made 3 days ahead; store, covered, in the fridge. To save time, you can use 100g (3 ounces) canned baby beets for the hummus. Wraps can be filled a few hours before serving; they are ideal to take to work for lunch.

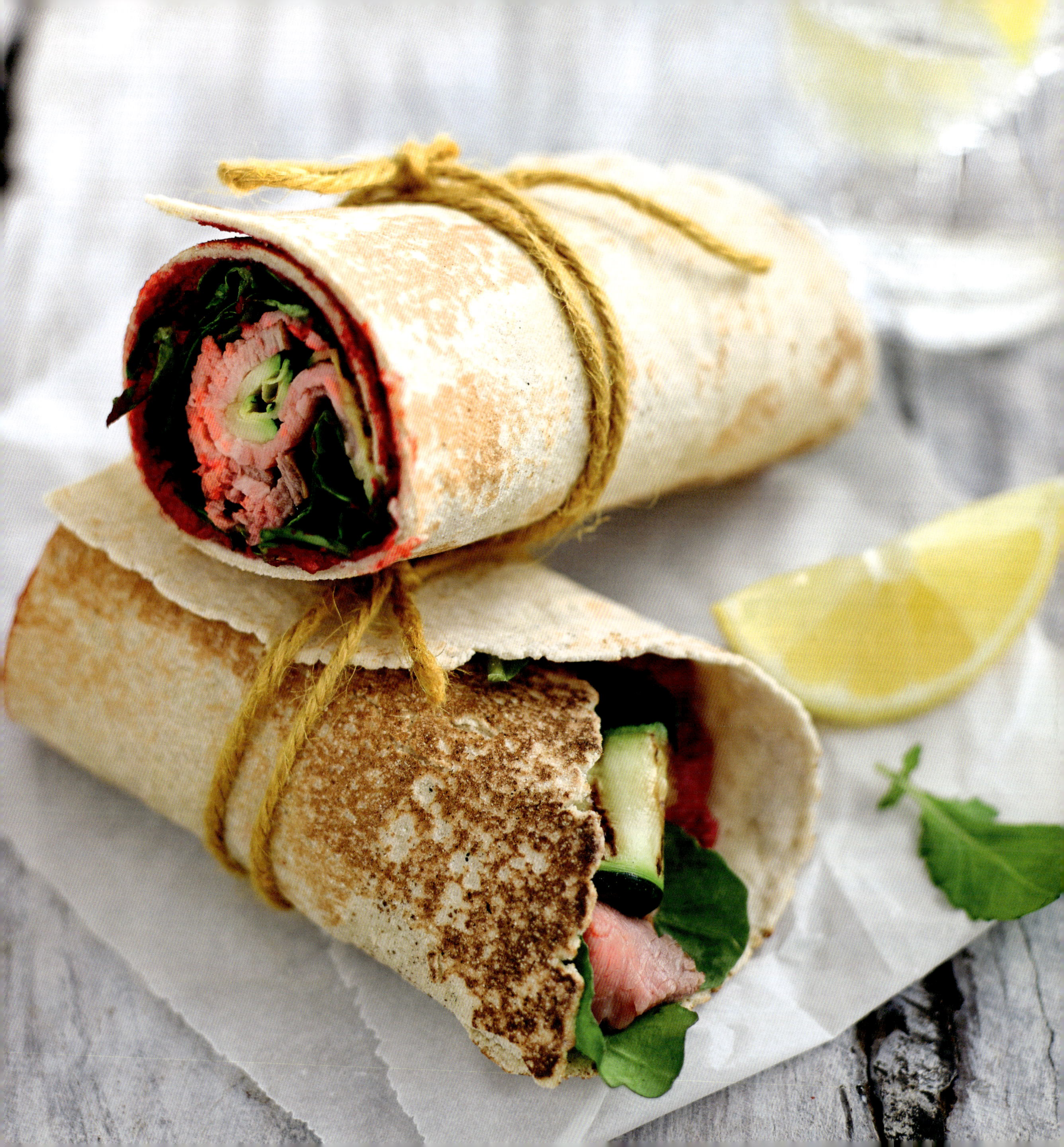

GLUTEN FREE · DAIRY FREE · NUT FREE

CHAR-GRILLED VEGETABLES AND PUMPKIN DIP ROLLS

PREP TIME 15 MINUTES **MAKES** 2

Drain a 280g (9-ounce) jar char-grilled vegetables; pat dry with paper towel, season. Sandwich ⅓ cup gluten-free moroccan pumpkin dip, char-grilled vegetables and 20g (¾ ounce) baby rocket leaves between 2 gluten-free torpedo rolls.

nutritional count per roll 20.9g total fat (2.1g saturated fat); 1488kJ (355 cal); 34g carbohydrate; 7.1g protein; 1.8g fibre

tip Use your favourite brand of gluten-free bread or make the recipe on page 58.

USE YOUR FAVOURITE BRAND OF GLUTEN-FREE BREAD OR MAKE THE RECIPE ON PAGE 58. WE USED SKINLESS BARBECUED CHICKEN BREASTS. USE A VEGETABLE PEELER TO SLICE RIBBONS FROM THE CARROT AND CUCUMBER.

GLUTEN FREE • DAIRY FREE • NUT FREE

CHICKEN, AVOCADO AND VEGETABLE ROLLS

PREP TIME 20 MINUTES **MAKES** 2

Combine ⅓ cup coarsely chopped fresh coriander, 2 tablespoons chopped fresh mint, 2 teaspoons finely grated lemon rind and 1 tablespoon each of lemon juice and grapeseed oil in a small bowl; season. Sandwich ½ medium mashed avocado, 1 cup sliced cooked chicken, 1 lebanese cucumber and 1 carrot sliced into ribbons, and herb mixture between two halved small gluten-free rolls.

nutritional count per roll 27.8g total fat (5.3g saturated fat); 2045kJ (489 cal); 29.2g carbohydrate; 27g protein; 7.4g fibre

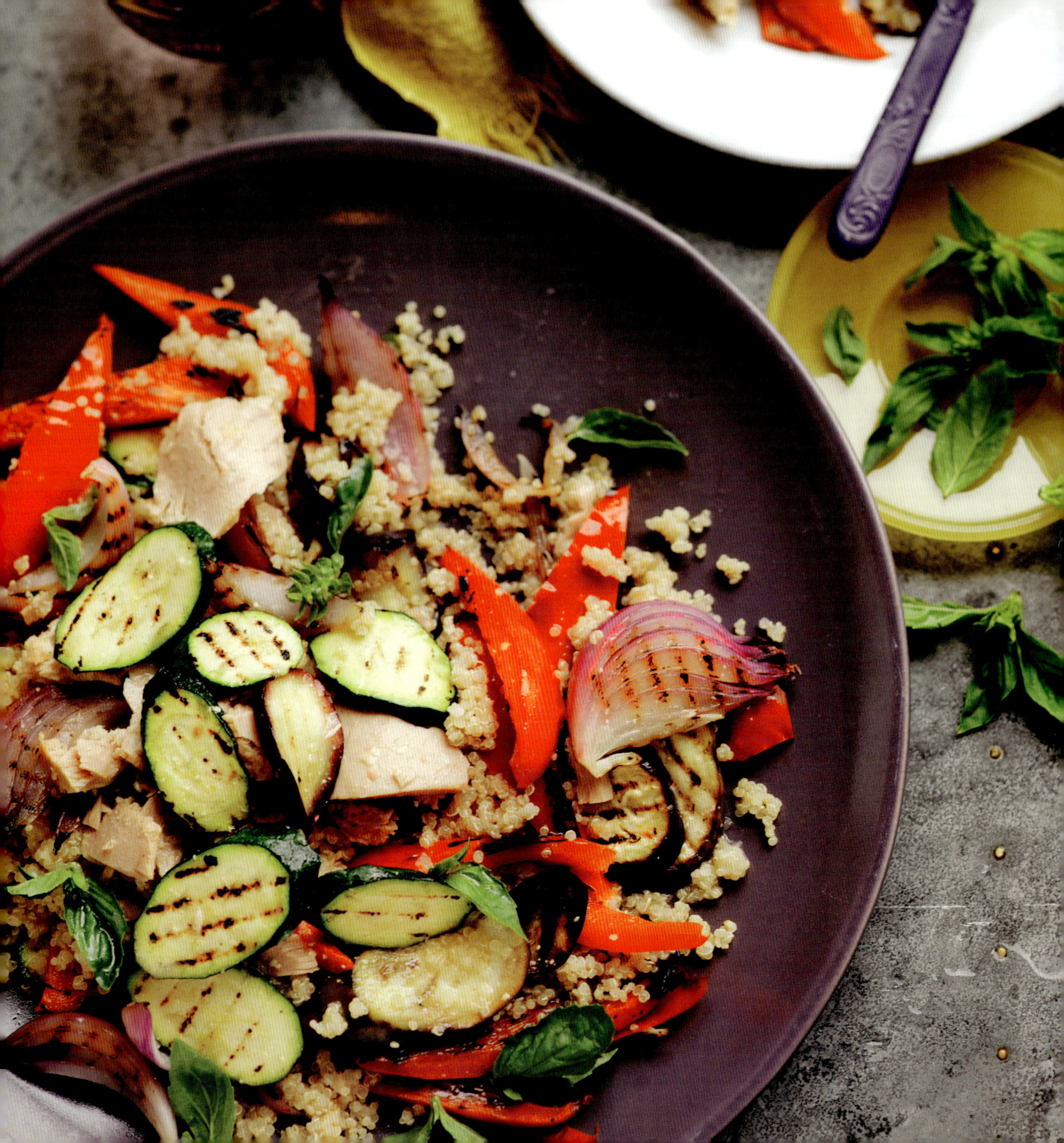

GLUTEN FREE • DAIRY FREE • EGG FREE • NUT FREE

QUINOA SALAD WITH VEGETABLES AND TUNA

PREP + COOK TIME 25 MINUTES SERVES 4

1 medium red capsicum (bell pepper) (200g), quartered

2 medium zucchini (240g), sliced thinly

2 baby eggplant (120g), sliced thinly

1 medium red onion (170g), cut into wedges

⅔ cup (140g) quinoa, rinsed, drained

1⅓ cups (320ml) water

1 tablespoon olive oil

⅓ cup (80ml) lemon juice

2 teaspoons dijon mustard

425g (3½ ounces) canned tuna in springwater, drained

⅓ cup baby basil leaves

1 Cook capsicum, zucchini, eggplant and onion on a heated oiled grill plate (or grill or barbecue) until tender. Slice capsicum thickly.
2 Meanwhile, place quinoa in a small saucepan with the water; bring to the boil. Reduce heat to low; simmer, covered, for 15 minutes or until tender and water is absorbed. Remove from heat; stand for 10 minutes, then fluff with a fork.
3 Place oil, juice and mustard in a screw-top jar; shake well.
4 Place vegetables and quinoa in a bowl with tuna and dressing; toss gently to combine. Serve salad topped with basil.

nutritional count per serving 9.5g total fat (1.9g saturated fat); 1416kJ (338 cal); 29g carbohydrate; 30.6g protein; 5.7g fibre

tips Vegetables can be grilled a day ahead; store, covered, in the fridge. The salad can be served warm or cold; add some rocket (arugula) or spinach leaves, if you like.

GLUTEN FREE • EGG FREE • NUT FREE

SPICED LENTIL AND ROASTED KUMARA SOUP

PREP + COOK TIME 45 MINUTES SERVES 4

1 large kumara (orange sweet potato) (500g), cut into 2cm (¾-inch) cubes

cooking-oil spray

1 medium brown onion (150g), chopped coarsely

1 clove garlic, crushed

1 cup (250ml) gluten-free vegetable stock

1 teaspoon ground cumin

1 teaspoon ground coriander

½ teaspoon ground turmeric

½ cup (100g) dried red lentils, rinsed

1 litre (4 cups) water

⅔ cup (95g) low-fat gluten-free plain yoghurt

¼ cup finely chopped fresh coriander (cilantro)

1 Preheat oven to 220°C/425°F. Place kumara on a baking-paper-lined oven tray; spray with oil. Bake for 25 minutes or until golden and tender.
2 Meanwhile, cook onion, garlic and 2 tablespoons of the stock in a medium saucepan over high heat, stirring, for 3 minutes or until onion is tender. Add spices; cook, stirring, for 30 seconds or until fragrant. Stir in lentils, remaining stock and the water; bring to the boil. Reduce heat; simmer, uncovered, 15 minutes or until lentils are tender. Add kumara; cook 5 minutes. Remove from heat; cool 10 minutes.
3 Blend or process mixture in batches until smooth. Return mixture to pan; stir over heat until hot.
4 Combine yoghurt and coriander in a small bowl. Serve soup topped with yoghurt mixture and extra coriander leaves, if you like.

nutritional count per serving 2.7g total fat (0.5g saturated fat); 877kJ (209 cal); 30.9g carbohydrate; 12g protein; 6.7g fibre

tips Soup can be made a day ahead; store, covered, in the fridge. Freeze the soup without the yoghurt mixture in an airtight container for up to 3 months. Defrost in the fridge overnight then reheat in a small saucepan on the stove over medium heat for about 10 minutes or until hot.

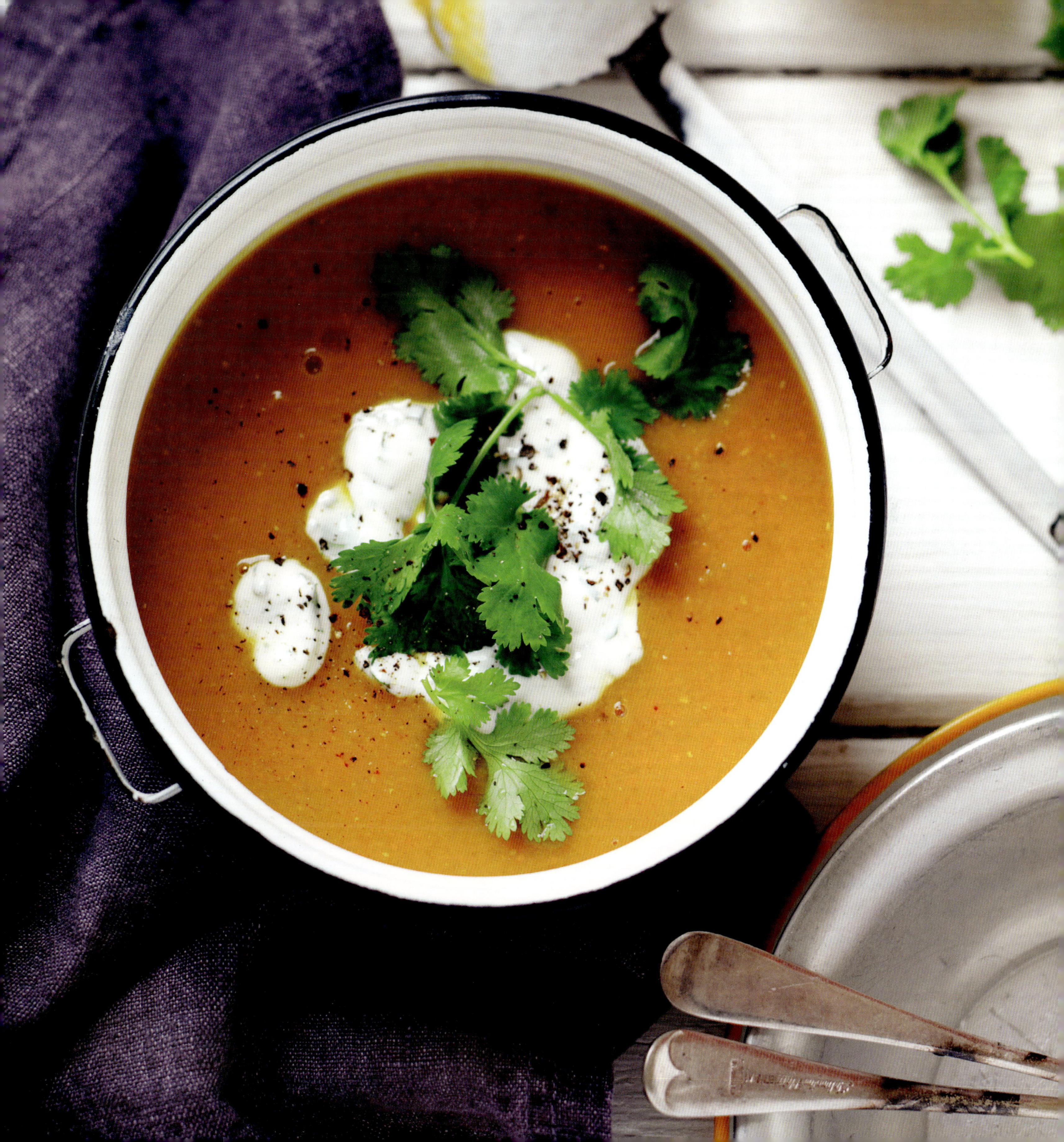

This recipe is perfect for any lunchbox as you can make it the night before; store, covered, in the fridge. If you're short on time, try making this salad with quinoa instead of rice; it will take less than half the time to cook and has a great fibre content, just like brown rice. You could use chicken breast or lamb fillets instead of the turkey.

LUNCH

GLUTEN FREE • EGG FREE

TURKEY AND BROWN RICE SALAD

PREP + COOK TIME 45 MINUTES SERVES 4

1⅓ cups (200g) brown rice

200g (6½ ounces) green beans, trimmed, halved lengthways

400g (12½ ounces) turkey breast steaks

6 red radishes (210g), sliced thinly

1 lebanese cucumber (130g), halved, sliced thinly

2 green onions (scallions), sliced thinly

2 trimmed celery stalks (200g), sliced thinly

80g (2½ ounces) goat's cheese, crumbled

2 tablespoons cashews, toasted, chopped coarsely

100g (3 ounces) baby rocket (arugula) leaves

½ cup loosely packed torn fresh basil leaves

2 tablespoons olive oil

⅓ cup (80ml) lemon juice

1 Place rice in a medium saucepan, cover with water; bring to the boil. Reduce heat; simmer, uncovered, for 35 minutes or until tender. Drain; rinse under cold water. Drain well.

2 Meanwhile, cook beans in a small saucepan of boiling water for 3 minutes or until just tender. Drain; refresh under cold water, drain.

3 Cook turkey on a heated oiled grill pan (or grill or barbecue) for 3 minutes each side or until cooked through. Cover; rest for 5 minutes, then slice thickly.

4 Combine rice, beans, turkey, radish, cucumber, onion, celery, goat's cheese, nuts, rocket and basil in a large bowl. Drizzle with combined oil and juice; toss to combine.

nutritional count per serving 21.2g total fat (5.9g saturated fat); 2150kJ (513 cal); 44.5g carbohydrate;

GLUTEN FREE • DAIRY FREE • EGG FREE • NUT FREE

HOT AND SOUR PRAWN AND CHICKEN SOUP

PREP + COOK TIME 30 MINUTES SERVES 4

1.5 litres (6 cups) water
4 fresh kaffir lime leaves, torn
80g (2½ ounces) fresh ginger, sliced thickly
1 fresh small red thai (serrano) chilli, sliced thinly
200g (6½ ounces) dried rice noodles
8 green king prawns (shrimp) (280g)
200g (6½ ounces) chicken breast, sliced thinly
2 tablespoons lime juice
200g (6½ ounces) snow peas, shredded
500g (1 pound) baby choy sum, trimmed, chopped
1 cup (80g) bean sprouts
½ cup loosely packed fresh coriander (cilantro) leaves
½ cup loosely packed fresh mint leaves
½ cup loosely packed fresh thai basil leaves

1 Combine the water, lime leaves, ginger and half the chilli in a medium saucepan over high heat; bring to the boil. Reduce heat; simmer, covered, for 10 minutes. Discard leaves and ginger.
2 Meanwhile, cook noodles in a medium saucepan of boiling water according to packet directions; drain.
3 Shell and devein prawns, leaving tails intact. Add prawns and chicken to broth; simmer for 5 minutes or until chicken and prawns are cooked. Stir in juice.
4 Divide noodles, snow peas and choy sum among four serving bowls; ladle over broth mixture. Top with sprouts, herbs and remaining chilli.

nutritional count per serving 3.8g total fat; (0.9g saturated fat); 1101kJ (263 cal); 28.4g carbohydrate; 25g protein; 5.8g fibre

tips Make sure the broth is piping hot so it will slightly cook the choy sum and snow peas. If you can't find baby choy sum, use ½ bunch of normal choy sum or another asian green. Kaffir lime leaves are sold in small packets. Freeze the remaining leaves – they lose a bit of colour but keep all their flavour. You can use a gluten-free chicken stock instead of the water, if you like.

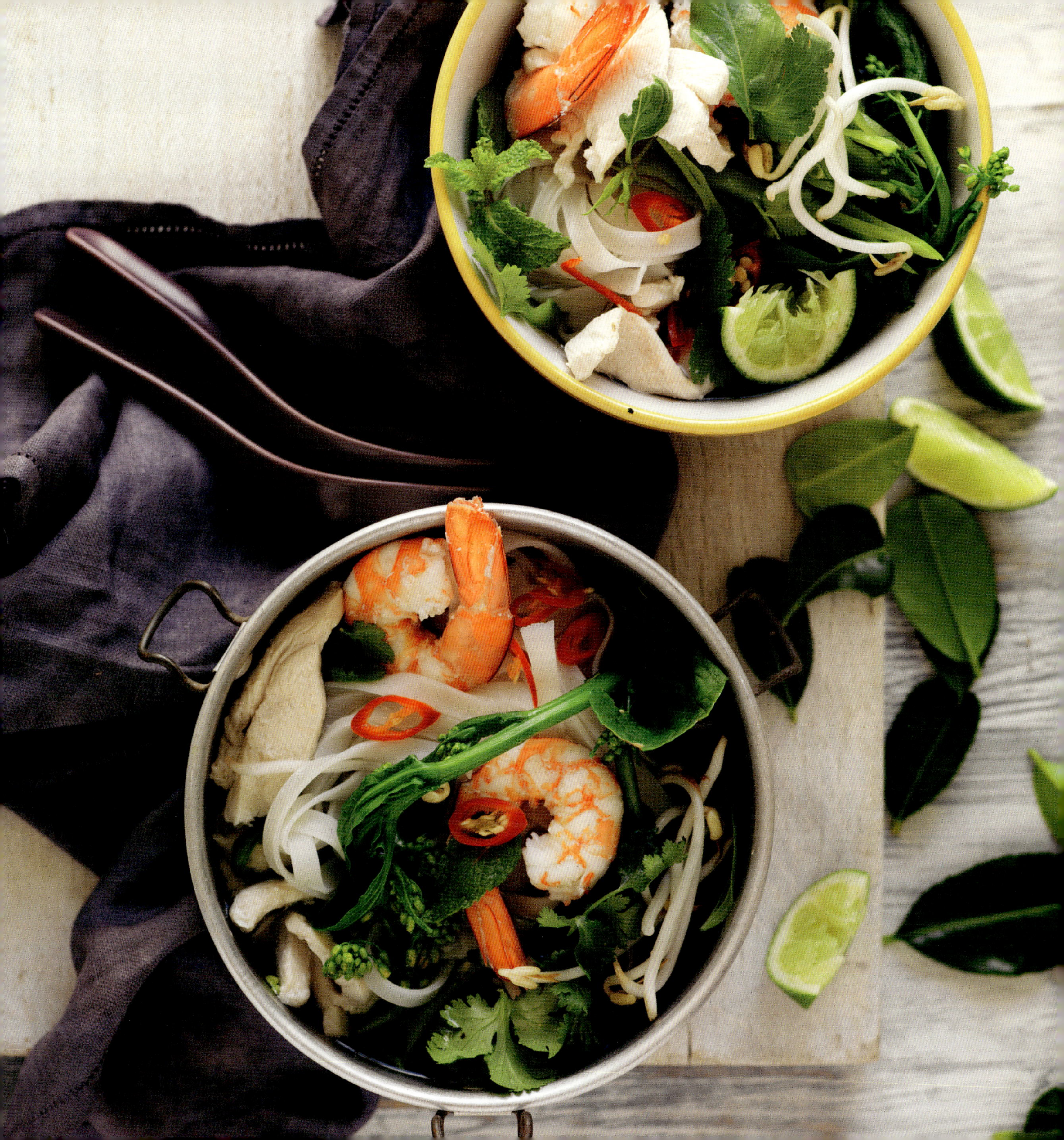

PURCHASE SASHIMI GRADE TUNA FOR THIS RECIPE.
SWAP THE TUNA FOR SALMON IF YOU LIKE.
IF THE CHERMOULA INGREDIENTS AREN'T BLENDING WELL,
ADD 1 TABLESPOON WATER TO THE MIXTURE.

LUNCH

GLUTEN FREE • DAIRY FREE • EGG FREE • NUT FREE

CHERMOULA TUNA, CHICKPEA AND BROAD BEAN SALAD

PREP + COOK TIME 30 MINUTES (+ REFRIGERATION) SERVES 4

400g (12½-ounce) piece tuna steak
2 cup (300g) frozen broad (fava) beans
200g (6½ ounces) green beans, trimmed, cut into thirds
840g (1¾ pounds) canned chickpeas (garbanzo beans), drained, rinsed
1 cup firmly packed fresh flat-leaf parsley leaves
2 medium lemons (280g), segmented (see tip)
2 tablespoons lemon juice
2 tablespoons olive oil

CHERMOULA
1 small red onion (100g), chopped coarsely
1 clove garlic, peeled
2 cup firmly packed fresh coriander (cilantro) leaves, chopped coarsely
2 cup firmly packed fresh flat-leaf parsley leaves, chopped coarsely
2 teaspoons ground cumin
2 teaspoons smoked paprika
2 tablespoons olive oil

1 Make chermoula; reserve three-quarters to serve.
2 Place tuna in a shallow dish with remaining chermoula; toss to coat. Cover; refrigerate 30 minutes.
3 Meanwhile, place broad beans in a heatproof bowl, cover with boiling water; stand for 2 minutes. Rinse under cold water; drain. Peel beans.
4 Boil, steam or microwave green beans until just tender; drain, rinse under cold water, drain.
5 Cook tuna on a heated oiled grill plate (or grill or barbecue) for 2 minutes each side or until slightly charred on the outside but still rare in the centre. Cover; stand for 5 minutes. Slice tuna, across the grain.
6 Combine broad beans, green beans, chickpeas, parsley and lemon segments in a medium bowl with combined juice and oil. Serve tuna with salad and top with reserved chermoula.

CHERMOULA Blend or process ingredients until just combined.

nutritional count per serving 23.6g total fat; (3.7g saturated fat); 2208kJ (527 cal); 29.6g carbohydrate; 43.7g protein; 18.1g fibre

tip To segment the lemons, cut off the rind with the white pith, following the curve of the fruit. Cut down either side of each segment close to the membrane to release the segment.

LUNCH

GLUTEN FREE • DAIRY FREE • NUT FREE

VIETNAMESE PANCAKES WITH PRAWNS

PREP + COOK TIME 30 MINUTES SERVES 4

16 cooked tiger prawns (shrimp) (560g)

1 cup (180g) rice flour

½ teaspoon ground turmeric

⅓ cup (80ml) reduced-fat coconut milk

1⅓ cups (330ml) water

2 eggs

2 tablespoons olive oil

16 butter (boston) lettuce leaves (from the centre of the lettuce)

2 lebanese cucumber (260g), sliced into ribbons

2 medium carrots (240g), sliced into ribbons

2 cups (160g) bean sprouts

1 bunch fresh mint leaves

1 bunch fresh thai basil leaves

CHILLI DIPPING SAUCE

2 tablespoons warm water

2 tablespoons lemon juice

1 tablespoon caster (superfine) sugar

1 teaspoon fish sauce

1 clove garlic, crushed

1 fresh small red thai chilli (serrano), chopped finely

1 Make chilli dipping sauce.
2 Shell and devein prawns, leaving tails intact.
3 Place rice flour and turmeric in a medium bowl. Whisk in coconut milk, the water and eggs until well combined and batter is smooth.
4 Heat 1 teaspoon of the oil in a large non-stick frying pan (base measurement 23cm/9 inches) over medium heat; pour a quarter of the batter into pan, swirl around base to form a thin pancake. Cook for 2 minutes or until batter has set. Slide pancake onto a serving plate. Repeat to make eight pancakes in total.
5 Serve pancakes with lettuce, prawns, cucumber, carrot, sprouts, herbs and chilli dipping sauce.

CHILLI DIPPING SAUCE Stir the water, juice and sugar in a small bowl until sugar has dissolved. Add remaining ingredients; stir to combine.

nutritional count per serving 14.7g total fat (3.9g saturated fat); 1800kJ (430 cal); 47.1g carbohydrate; 23.5g protein; 6.5g fibre

This traditional Vietnamese lunch is eaten by tearing off a piece of pancake and placing it inside a lettuce leaf, along with some prawns, vegetables, sprouts and herbs; it is then rolled up and dipped into a sauce. Use a vegetable peeler to slice thin ribbons from the cucumber and carrot.

DINNER

BEFORE YOU START BASIC STEPS

SHALLOW FRYING SCHNITZELS
Heat enough oil to coat the base of a large frying pan and shallow-fry the schnitzels turning once until golden brown and cooked through. Transfer schnitzels to a plate lined with paper towel to drain off any excess oil.

SHAPING GNOCCHI
Roll each piece of gnocchi dough into balls. Roll each ball along the tines of a fork, pressing lightly on top of the ball with your index finger to form a classic gnocchi shape, with grooves on one side and a dimple on the other.

DINNER

PREPARING ASPARAGUS
Snap the woody end off asparagus spears by holding it close to the base then bending it until it snaps. Discard the woody end. Use a vegetable peeler to neaten the end of the spear.

CUTTING CARROTS INTO MATCHSTICKS (JULIENNE)
Cut the peeled carrot in half crossways, then into thin slices lengthways; cut the slices into thin matchsticks. You can trim the carrot into a rectangular shape first, if you like; this will make it more secure on the cutting board.

DINNER

GLUTEN FREE • DAIRY FREE • EGG FREE • NUT FREE

PEANUT-FREE SATAY CHICKEN SKEWERS

PREP + COOK TIME 30 MINUTES SERVES 4

We used a peanut-butter-style, nut-free butter made from roasted sunflower seeds; available smooth and crunchy, from healthfood stores, some larger supermarkets and online. You need to cook ⅔ cup jasmine rice for the amount of cooked rice needed.

⅓ cup (95g) nut-free butter
270ml (8½ ounces) canned coconut milk
2 tablespoons tamari
2 tablespoons sweet chilli sauce
2 tablespoons lime juice
2 tablespoons tamari, extra
1 teaspoon sweet chilli sauce, extra
12 chicken tenderloins (640g)
200g (6½ ounces) snow peas, trimmed, sliced
2 cups (300g) cooked jasmine rice
2 tablespoons fresh coriander (cilantro) leaves

1 Heat a small heavy-based saucepan over medium heat; cook nut-free butter and coconut milk, without boiling, stirring until smooth. Stir in tamari, sweet chilli sauce and juice; cook, stirring for 1 minute or until hot.
2 Combine extra tamari and extra sweet chilli sauce in a small bowl. Thread chicken onto 12 skewers; season. Cook chicken on a heated, oiled grill pan (or barbecue or grill) for about 2 minutes each side or until cooked through; brush with half the tamari mixture in the final minute of cooking.
3 Meanwhile, boil, steam or microwave snow peas until just tender. Combine snow peas with remaining tamari mixture until coated.
4 Serve chicken on rice with snow peas and satay sauce; sprinkle with coriander.

nutritional count per serving 35g total fat (16.5g saturated fat); 2737kJ (654 cal); 36.8g carbohydrate; 46.1g protein; 2.9g fibre

serving suggestion Serve with stir-fried asian greens.

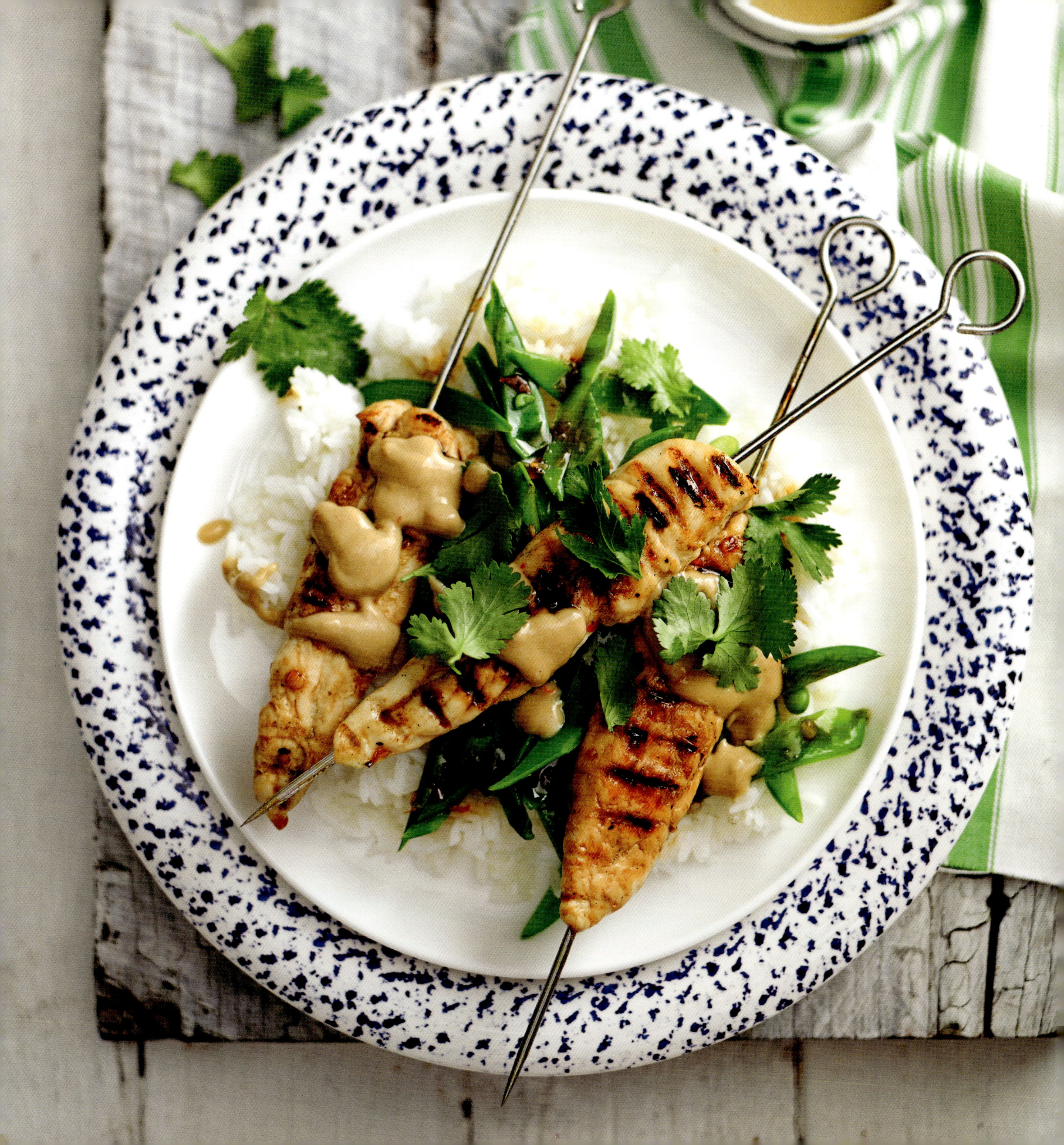

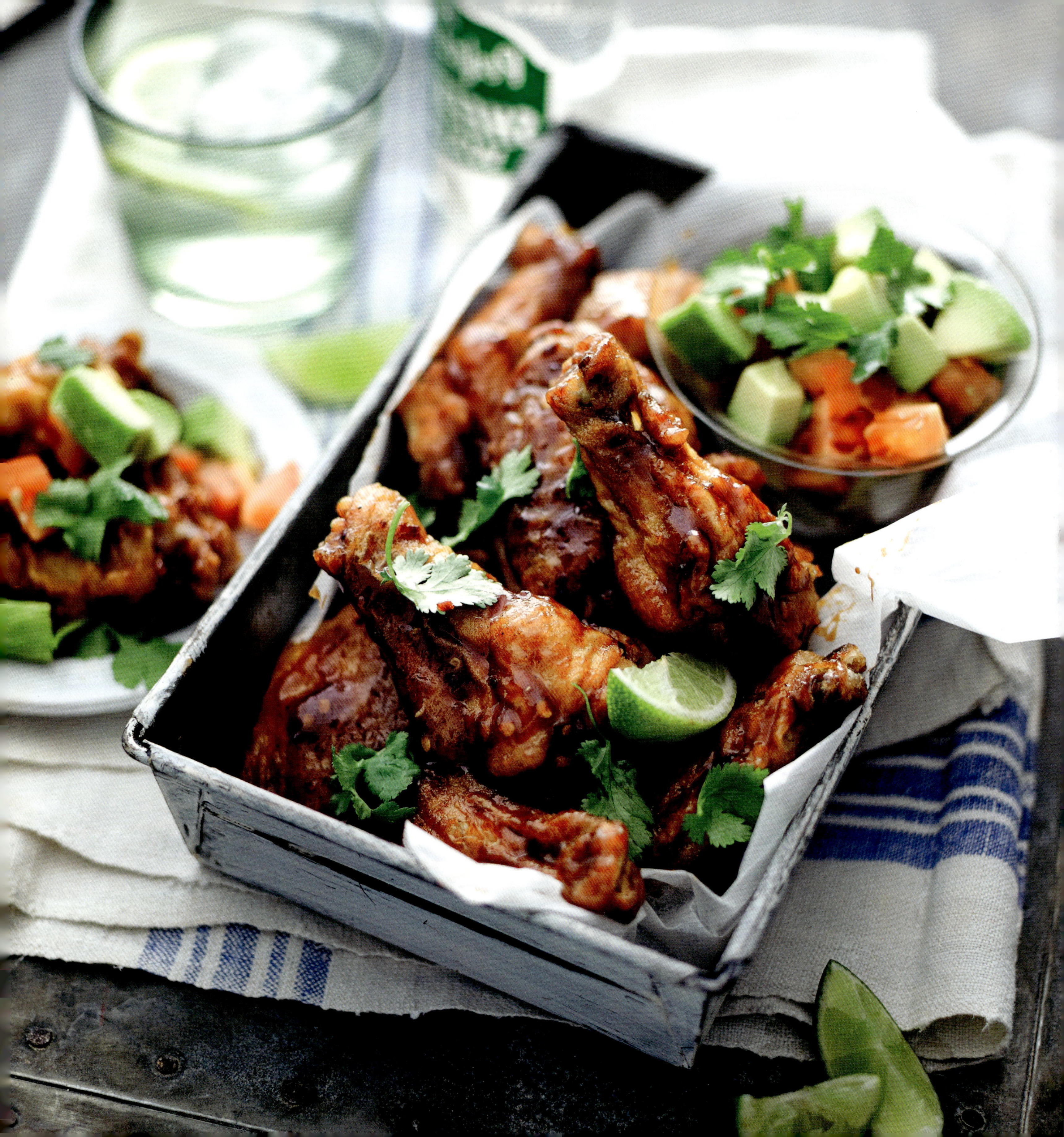

DINNER

GLUTEN FREE • DAIRY FREE • EGG FREE • NUT FREE

SOUTHERN BUFFALO-STYLE CHICKEN WINGS

PREP + COOK TIME 1¼ HOURS SERVES 4

16 chicken wings (2kg)
1 cup (180g) rice flour
⅓ cup (95g) gluten-free tomato sauce (ketchup)
¼ cup (70g) gluten-free barbecue sauce
1½ tablespoons white vinegar
1 teaspoon chilli flakes

TOMATO AVOCADO SALSA
2 large tomatoes (500g), chopped coarsely
1 large avocado (320g), chopped coarsely
2 tablespoons lemon juice
⅓ cup coarsely chopped fresh coriander (cilantro)

1 Preheat oven to 220°C/425°F. Oil two wire racks; place over two large baking trays.
2 Cut wings into three pieces at the joints; discard wing tips. Toss wings in rice flour; place on wire racks. Bake, uncovered, for 40 minutes, turning once during cooking, until golden brown and cooked through.
3 Meanwhile, make tomato avocado salsa.
4 Place sauces, vinegar and chilli flakes in a small saucepan; cook, stirring, over medium heat, until hot. Transfer sauce to a large bowl. Add hot chicken; toss until coated.
5 Serve chicken with tomato avocado salsa.

TOMATO AVOCADO SALSA Combine ingredients in a medium bowl.

nutritional count per serving 75.3g total fat (21.2g saturated fat); 5507kJ (1315 cal); 72.7g carbohydrate; 77.2g protein; 22.1g fibre

tips To save time, ask the butcher to remove the wing tips and cut the wings into two pieces. If you don't want spicy wings, add less chilli flakes, or omit the chilli altogether if serving for the whole family. This recipe is best made just before serving.

DINNER

GLUTEN FREE • DAIRY FREE • EGG FREE • YEAST FREE • NUT FREE

CHICKEN SCHNITZEL WITH CORN AND TOMATO SALAD

PREP + COOK TIME **1 HOUR** SERVES **4**

2 medium red capsicums (400g), chopped coarsely

200g (6½ ounces) red grape tomatoes

1½ tablespoons olive oil

2 trimmed corn cobs (500g)

4 chicken breast fillets (800g)

½ cup (125ml) soy milk

2 teaspoons smoked paprika

1 cup (100g) quinoa flakes

1 tablespoon finely chopped fresh lemon thyme

vegetable oil, for shallow frying

1 tablespoon red wine vinegar

1 teaspoon dijon mustard

2 green onions (scallions), sliced thinly

½ cup loosely packed fresh coriander (cilantro) leaves

1 Preheat oven to 160°C/325°F.
2 Place capsicum and tomatoes in a roasting pan; drizzle with 2 teaspoons of the olive oil. Roast for 20 minutes or until tomatoes begin to soften.
3 Meanwhile, cook corn on a heated oiled grill plate (or barbecue or grill), turning occasionally, 15 minutes or until corn is lightly charred and tender. Cool slightly. When cool enough to handle, cut down the cobs with a sharp knife to remove the kernels. Place in a large bowl.
4 Using a sharp knife, cut each chicken breast in half widthways. Place a chicken half between two pieces of plastic wrap; gently pound with a meat mallet or rolling pin until 1cm (½-inch) thick. Repeat with remaining chicken halves.
5 Combine soy milk and 1 teaspoon of paprika in a medium bowl, season; add chicken, toss to coat.
6 Combine quinoa, thyme and remaining paprika in a large shallow bowl. Remove chicken, one piece at a time, from milk mixture; gently shake off excess, dip into quinoa mixture to coat.
7 Heat enough vegetable oil in a large frying pan to come 2cm (¾-inch) up the side of the pan; cook chicken, in batches, over medium-high heat, for 2 minutes each side or until chicken is golden brown and cooked through. Drain on paper towel.
8 Place vinegar, mustard and remaining olive oil in a screw-top jar; shake well, season to taste.
9 Add capsicum mixture to corn with green onion, coriander and dressing; toss gently to combine. Serve chicken with salad.

nutritional count per serving 40.2g total fat (7.5g saturated fat); 3135kJ (749 cal); 40.1g carbohydrate; 53.6g protein; 7.3g fibre

CHICKEN CAN BE COATED IN QUINOA MIXTURE A DAY AHEAD; STORE, COVERED, IN THE FRIDGE. IF YOU DON'T HAVE A DAIRY ALLERGY, USE BUTTERMILK INSTEAD OF THE SOY MILK.

TO SAVE YOU TIME, ASK THE FISHMONGER TO CLEAN THE SQUID HOODS FOR YOU. THIS RECIPE IS BEST MADE JUST BEFORE SERVING.

GLUTEN FREE • DAIRY FREE • EGG FREE • YEAST FREE • NUT FREE

SALT AND PEPPER SQUID

PREP + COOK TIME 35 MINUTES SERVES 4

2 tablespoons sea salt

2 tablespoons black peppercorns

1½ teaspoons dried chilli flakes

¼ cup (35g) 100% corn (maize) cornflour (cornstarch)

vegetable oil, for deep frying

3 whole squid (1.5kg), cleaned, slice thickly

125g (4 ounces) mixed baby salad leaves

1 lebanese cucumber (130g), halved, sliced thinly

½ cup loosely packed fresh coriander (cilantro) leaves

½ small red onion (50g), sliced thinly

1 small carrot (70g), cut into matchsticks

1 tablespoon rice wine vinegar

2 teaspoons light olive oil

1 Crush salt, peppercorns and chilli with a mortar and pestle; combine with cornflour in a medium bowl.

2 Heat vegetable oil in a large heavy-based saucepan over medium-high heat until oil reaches 190°C/375°F on a sugar (candy) thermometer (or when a cube of bread turns golden in about 10 seconds).

3 Coat squid in cornflour mixture; shake off excess. Deep-fry squid, in batches, for 3 minutes or until lightly browned and cooked through. Drain on paper towel; cover to keep warm.

4 Place salad leaves and remaining ingredients in a large bowl; toss gently to combine. Serve squid with salad and, if you like, lemon wedges.

nutritional count per serving 15.6g total fat (2.4g saturated fat); 1213kJ (290 cal); 11.3g carbohydrate; 32.6g protein; 2.9g fibre

DINNER

GLUTEN FREE • DAIRY FREE • EGG FREE • YEAST FREE • NUT FREE

SALMON AND QUINOA KOFTA WITH HERB TOMATO SALAD

PREP + COOK TIME 45 MINUTES (+ COOLING) SERVES 4

We used red quinoa in this recipe, but you could use the white variety if you prefer.

½ cup (100g) quinoa

1 cup (250ml) water

600g (1¼ pounds) salmon fillets, skin and bones removed, chopped coarsely

1 medium brown onion (150g), grated coarsely

2 teaspoons ground cumin

1 teaspoon ground coriander

1 teaspoon ground cinnamon

1 teaspoon ground allspice

1 tablespoon olive oil

HERB TOMATO SALAD

500g (1 pound) mixed tomato medley, sliced thickly

1 medium red onion (170g), sliced thinly

½ cup loosely packed fresh flat-leaf parsley leaves

½ cup loosely packed fresh mint leaves

2 tablespoons pomegranate molasses

2 tablespoons olive oil

1 Rinse quinoa under cold running water until liquid runs clear; drain well. Place quinoa in a medium saucepan with the water; bring to the boil. Reduce heat to low; cook, covered, for 15 minutes or until liquid is absorbed. Cool.
2 Meanwhile, make herb tomato salad.
3 Blend or process salmon until finely chopped; transfer to a medium bowl. Add quinoa, onion and spices; season, stir to combine. Shape mixture into 12 oval shapes.
4 Heat oil in a large frying pan over medium heat; cook kofta, in two batches, turning, for 3 minutes or until golden brown and just cooked through. Remove from pan, cover; rest for 5 minutes.
5 Serve kofta with herb tomato salad.

HERB TOMATO SALAD Place tomatoes, onion and herbs in a large bowl with combined pomegranate molasses and oil; toss to combine, season to taste.

nutritional count per serving 16.2g total fat (2.6g saturated fat); 1556kJ (372 cal); 35g carbohydrate; 19.2g protein; 5.1g fibre

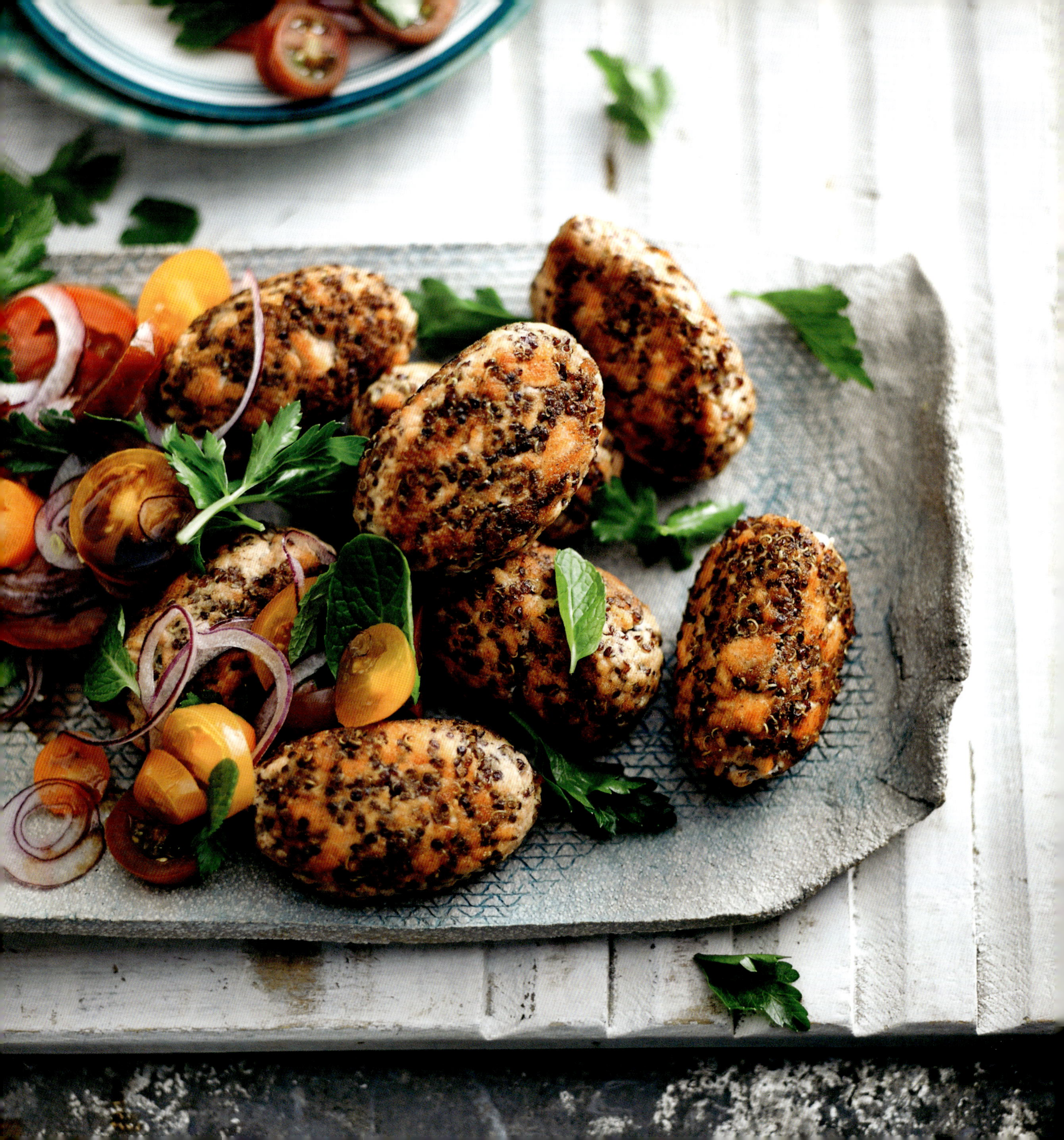

We used sebago potatoes for this recipe – a dry floury potato, that holds its shape well when boiled. Both the gnocchi and the rocket pesto can be made a day ahead; store separately, covered, in the fridge. Swap the rocket for baby spinach leaves, if you like.

DINNER

GLUTEN FREE • EGG FREE • NUT FREE

POTATO AND PUMPKIN GNOCCHI WITH ROCKET PESTO

PREP + COOK TIME 1¼ HOURS SERVES 4

3 medium potatoes (600g), unpeeled (see tips)

800g (1½ pounds) pumpkin, cut into cubes

3 teaspoons olive oil

⅓ cup (25g) finely grated parmesan

⅔ cup (90g) gluten-free plain (all-purpose) flour, approximately

15g (½ ounce) baby rocket (arugula) leaves

ROCKET PESTO

1 cup loosely packed fresh basil leaves

15g (½ ounce) baby rocket (arugula) leaves

½ cup (40g) finely grated parmesan

1 clove garlic, crushed

⅓ cup (80ml) olive oil

1 Preheat oven to 180°C/375°F.
2 Prick unpeeled potatoes with a fork. Place on a baking tray; roast for 45 minutes.
3 Place pumpkin on a baking-paper-lined oven tray; drizzle with 1 teaspoon of the oil, season and toss to coat. Roast, alongside potato, for final 30 minutes of potato cooking time, or until potato and pumpkin are tender.
4 Meanwhile, make rocket pesto; season.
5 When cool enough to handle, peel potatoes. Using a ricer, mouli or a fine sieve and a wooden spoon, mash potato and half the pumpkin in a large bowl until very smooth; season. Stir in cheese and ½ cup of the flour to make a firm dough. Add remaining flour only if needed.
6 Divide dough into 4 equal portions. Roll each portion on a gluten-free-floured surface into 2cm (¾-inch) thick sausage shapes; cut each into 3cm (1¼-inch) pieces, roll into balls. Roll each ball along the tines of a fork, pressing lightly on top of ball with your index finger to form a classic gnocchi shape, with grooves on one side and a dimple on the other.
7 Cook gnocchi, in three batches, in a large saucepan of boiling water, uncovered, 2 minutes or until gnocchi float to the surface. Continue cooking for 2 minutes. Remove from pan with a slotted spoon; drain.
8 Heat remaining oil in a medium frying pan over high heat; cook gnocchi and remaining pumpkin, in two batches, stirring gently, for 2 minutes or until pumpkin is golden.
9 Return gnocchi and pumpkin to the pan; toss through rocket pesto. Serve gnocchi with baby rocket leaves and, if you like, sprinkle with shaved parmesan.

ROCKET PESTO Process basil, rocket, parmesan and garlic until finely chopped. With motor operating, add oil in a thin, steady stream; process until combined.

nutritional count per serving 27.5g total fat (6.4g saturated fat); 2105kJ (503 cal); 48.6g carbohydrate; 12.1g protein; 7g fibre

DINNER

GLUTEN FREE • DAIRY FREE • EGG FREE • NUT FREE

SMOKED TROUT, PEA AND ASPARAGUS RISOTTO

PREP + COOK TIME 45 MINUTES SERVES 4

1 litre (4 cups) gluten-free vegetable stock
2 cups (500ml) water
1 tablespoon olive oil
1 medium brown onion (150g), chopped finely
1½ cups (300g) arborio rice
170g (5½ ounces) asparagus, trimmed, cut into 4cm (1½-inch) pieces
100g (3 ounces) snow peas, sliced thinly lengthways
½ cup (60g) fresh or frozen peas
2 teaspoons finely grated lemon rind
2 tablespoons lemon juice
2 tablespoons finely chopped fresh chives
1 tablespoon coarsely chopped fresh dill
150g (4½ ounces) hot-smoked trout, flaked coarsely

1 Bring stock and the water to the boil in a small saucepan; reduce heat to low, simmer, covered.
2 Meanwhile, heat oil in a large saucepan over medium heat; cook onion, stirring, for 5 minutes or until soft. Add rice; stir to coat in onion mixture. Stir in 1 cup of the simmering stock mixture; cook, stirring, over low heat until liquid is absorbed.
3 Continue adding the simmering stock in ½-cup batches, stirring, until liquid is absorbed after each addition. Total cooking time should be about 20 minutes or until rice is tender.
4 Add asparagus, snow peas and peas to pan; cook, stirring, for 1 minute or until just tender. Remove from heat. Stir in rind, juice and herbs until just combined. Gently fold through trout, season. Serve risotto topped with a little extra dill and lemon rind, if you like.

nutritional count per serving 4.6g total fat (1g saturated fat); 1631kJ (389 cal); 65.8g carbohydrate; 18.8g protein; 3.2g fibre

tip Use a zesting tool to make the thin strips of lemon rind.

ADD MINT INSTEAD OF CHIVES OR DILL FOR A DIFFERENT FLAVOUR. TROUT CAN BE SWAPPED FOR HOT-SMOKED SALMON. THE RISOTTO IS BEST MADE JUST BEFORE SERVING.

Brush roti with garlic oil for a garlic flavour. Roti can be made a day ahead. To reheat, warm in a heated dry frying pan, or wrap in foil and place in a 180°C/350°F preheated oven for 10 minutes or until heated through.

DINNER

GLUTEN FREE • EGG FREE • YEAST FREE • NUT FREE

TANDOORI LAMB CUTLETS WITH GREEN ONION ROTI

PREP + COOK TIME 40 MINUTES (+ REFRIGERATION) SERVES 4

12 french-trimmed lamb cutlets (600g)

1 tablespoon tandoori paste

2 lebanese cucumbers (260g), sliced into ribbons

400g (12½ ounces) red radishes, sliced thinly

1 tablespoon white vinegar

1 tablespoon caster (superfine) sugar

1 cup loosely packed fresh mint leaves

1 cup loosely packed fresh coriander leaves (cilantro)

GREEN ONION ROTI

1 teaspoon cumin seeds

1 green onion (scallion), sliced thinly

1 cup (150g) chickpea (besan) flour

¼ teaspoon xantham gum

2 tablespoons buttermilk

2 tablespoons water

1 tablespoon vegetable oil

chickpea (besan) flour, extra, for dusting

2 tablespoons ghee, melted

1 Combine lamb and tandoori paste in a large bowl. Cover; refrigerate for 30 minutes.
2 Meanwhile, make green onion roti.
3 Place cucumber, radish, vinegar and sugar in a medium bowl; toss until sugar dissolves. Stand for 5 minutes to allow vegetables to pickle; drain. Add herbs; toss to combine.
4 Cook lamb on a heated oiled grill plate (or barbecue or grill) for 2 minutes each side or until cooked as desired. Cover lamb; rest for 5 minutes before serving with cucumber salad and roti.

GREEN ONION ROTI Stir cumin in a small dry frying pan, over medium heat, for 1 minute or until fragrant. Combine cumin, green onion, chickpea flour and xantham gum in a large bowl; season. Add buttermilk, the water and oil; stir to form a firm dough. Divide dough into eight balls. Flour work surface with extra chickpea flour; roll out each ball into 2mm (⅛-inch) thick, 12cm (4¾-inch) rounds. Brush a heated small frying pan with ghee; cook roti, over high heat, for 1 minute each side or until lightly golden and cooked through. Transfer to a plate, cover with foil to keep warm. Repeat with remaining roti dough and ghee.

nutritional count per serving 23.9g total fat (9.2g saturated fat); 1865kJ (446 cal); 28.8g carbohydrate; 25.2g protein; 8.2g fibre

DINNER

GLUTEN FREE • NUT FREE

PANCETTA AND MUSHROOM CRÊPES WITH TOMATO SAUCE

PREP + COOK TIME 1½ HOURS SERVES 4

1 tablespoon olive oil

1 large brown onion (200g), chopped finely

2 cloves garlic, crushed

400g (12½ ounces) canned diced tomatoes

2 tablespoons finely shredded fresh basil

200g (6½ ounces) button mushrooms, sliced thinly

50g (1½ ounces) mild pancetta, chopped coarsely

500g (1 pound) fresh ricotta

250g (8 ounces) frozen spinach, thawed, drained

1 cup (100g) coarsely grated mozzarella

GLUTEN-FREE CRÊPES

2 eggs

½ cup (65g) gluten-free plain (all-purpose) flour

¼ cup (45g) rice flour

¾ cup (180ml) milk

40g (1½ ounces) butter, melted

1 Make gluten-free crêpes.
2 Heat half the oil in a large frying pan over medium heat; cook onion and garlic, stirring, for 5 minutes or until onion softens. Add tomatoes; cook, uncovered, over low heat, stirring occasionally, for 5 minutes or until sauce thickens slightly. Remove from heat. Cool slightly. Stir in basil; season to taste.
3 Heat remaining oil in a medium frying pan over high heat; cook mushrooms and pancetta, stirring, for 5 minutes or until softened. Transfer to a medium bowl; stir in ricotta and spinach until combine. Season.
4 Preheat oven to 180°C/350°F.
5 Spoon half the tomato sauce over the base of a 2 litre (8-cup) ovenproof dish. Spoon ricotta mixture evenly over crêpes; roll to enclose. Arrange crêpes, side-by-side, in dish. Spoon over remaining tomato sauce; sprinkle with mozzarella.
6 Bake, uncovered, for 20 minutes or until mixture is heated through and mozzarella is golden.

GLUTEN-FREE CRÊPES Whisk eggs then both flours in a medium bowl. Gradually add milk, whisking between additions until batter is smooth; season. Heat a 20cm (8-inch) (base measurement) frying pan over medium heat; brush with melted butter. Pour 2 tablespoonfuls of batter into pan; swirl to coat base. Cook for 1 minute or until golden; turn, cook for a further 30 seconds. Repeat to make a total of eight crêpes.

nutritional count per serving 39.9g total fat (21g saturated fat); 2667kJ (637 cal); 33.8g carbohydrate; 34.5g protein; 7g fibre

CRÊPES CAN BE MADE A DAY AHEAD; STORE IN AN AIRTIGHT CONTAINER. SWAP PANCETTA FOR BACON OR HAM. FRESH RICOTTA IS AVAILABLE FROM THE DELI SECTION OF SUPERMARKETS.

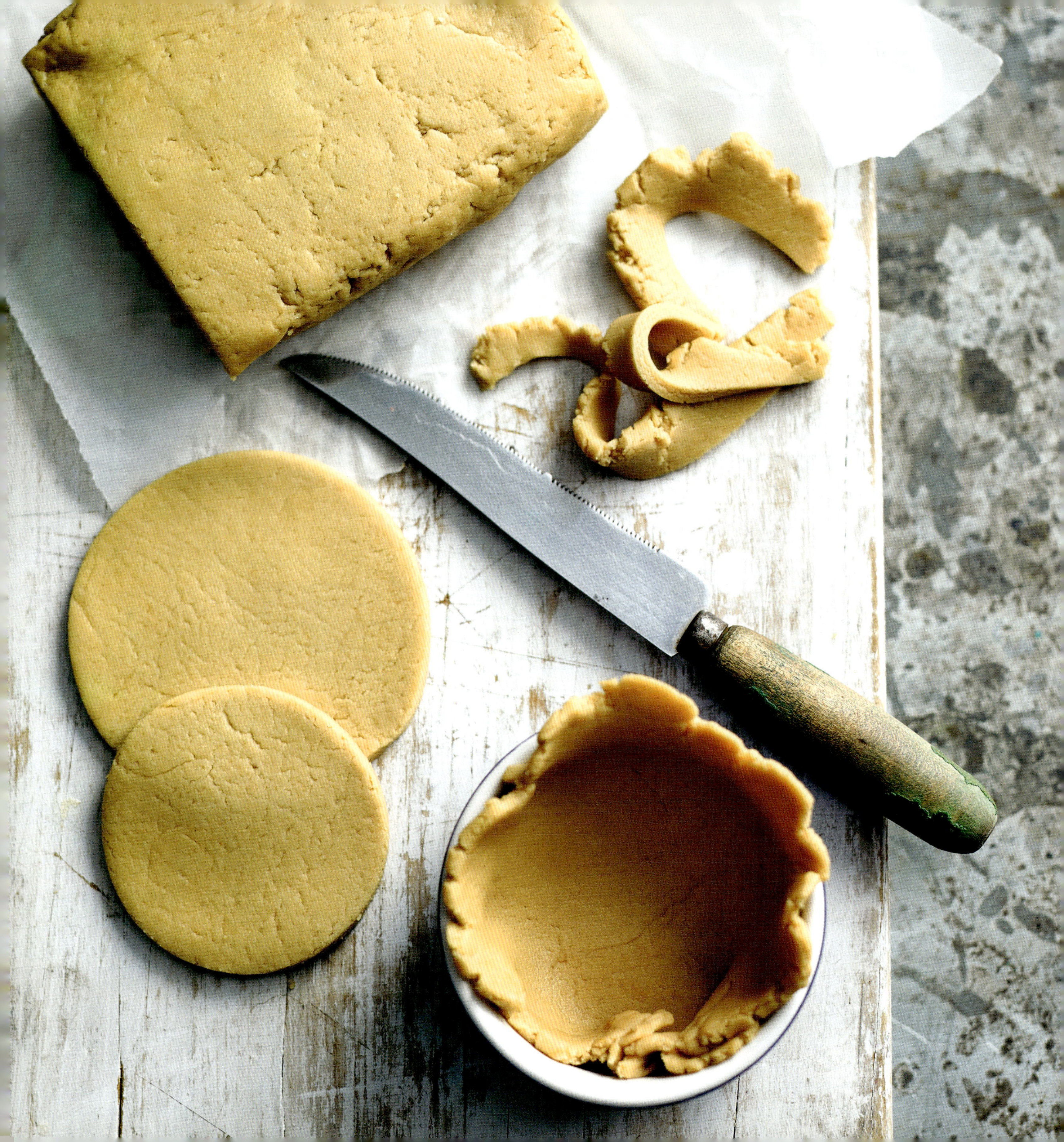

DINNER

GLUTEN FREE • EGG FREE • YEAST FREE • NUT FREE
GLUTEN-FREE PASTRY

PREP TIME 10 MINUTES **MAKES** 640G SHORTCRUST PASTRY

375g (12-ounce) packet gluten-free pastry mix

125g (4 ounces) cold butter, chopped coarsely

⅔ cup (160ml) water

2 tablespoons tamari

2 tablespoons olive oil

gluten-free plain (all-purpose) flour, for dusting

1 Place pastry mix in a large bowl; rub in butter until mixture resembles coarse breadcrumbs. Add enough of the combined water, tamari and oil until mixture comes together. Lightly knead on a surface dusted with a little gluten-free flour into a ball.
2 Roll pastry between two sheets of baking paper until 5mm (¼-inch) thick. Pastry is now ready to use.

nutritional count per quantity 142.6g total fat (73g saturated fat); 10744kJ (2567 cal); 30.2g carbohydrate; 13.3g protein; 7.5g fibre

tips Pastry is best used straight away. Rolling the pastry between sheets of baking paper will prevent the dough from sticking to the bench. If pastry dries out while you are using it, add a little olive oil to the dough. If pastry cracks when you are rolling it out or placing it into tart cases etc, it can quickly and easily be pushed back together without ruining it.

DINNER

GLUTEN FREE • EGG FREE • YEAST FREE • NUT FREE

SAUSAGE ROLLS

PREP + COOK TIME 1 HOUR (+ REFRIGERATION) MAKES 6

2 teaspoons olive oil
1 small leek (200g), chopped finely
1 small carrot (70g), grated finely
1 clove garlic, crushed
300g (9½ ounces) sausage mince
½ teaspoon roast lamb seasoning
1 tablespoon tomato paste
1½ rolls (600g) packaged sour cream gluten-free shortcrust pastry (see tips)
gluten-free plain (all-purpose) flour, for dusting
3 teaspoons sesame seeds or poppy seeds

1 Heat oil in a medium frying pan over high heat; cook leek, carrot and garlic, stirring, for 5 minutes or until soft. Cool.
2 Combine mince, seasoning, paste and vegetable mixture in a medium bowl; season.
3 Roll pastry on a surface dusted with gluten-free flour until 4mm (¼ inch) thick; cut into six 12cm (6½-inch) squares. Spoon ⅓ cup of mixture down one edge of each square. Roll to enclose. Brush edges with a little water; press to seal. Score pastry with a sharp knife; sprinkle with seeds. Refrigerate for 30 minutes or until firm.
4 Preheat oven to 180°C/350°F. Oil a baking tray; line with baking paper. Place rolls on tray.
5 Bake rolls for 20 minutes or until pastry is browned lightly and filling is cooked through. Serve with mustard or gluten-free tomato sauce (ketchup).

nutritional count per roll 41.8g total fat (23.9g saturated fat); 2441kJ (583 cal); 35g carbohydrate; 15.8g protein; 1.3g fibre

tips Sour cream gluten-free shortcrust pastry comes in 400g (12½-ounce) rolls; it is available from most major supermarkets in the freezer section. If using the gluten-free pastry on page 105, you will need one quantity.

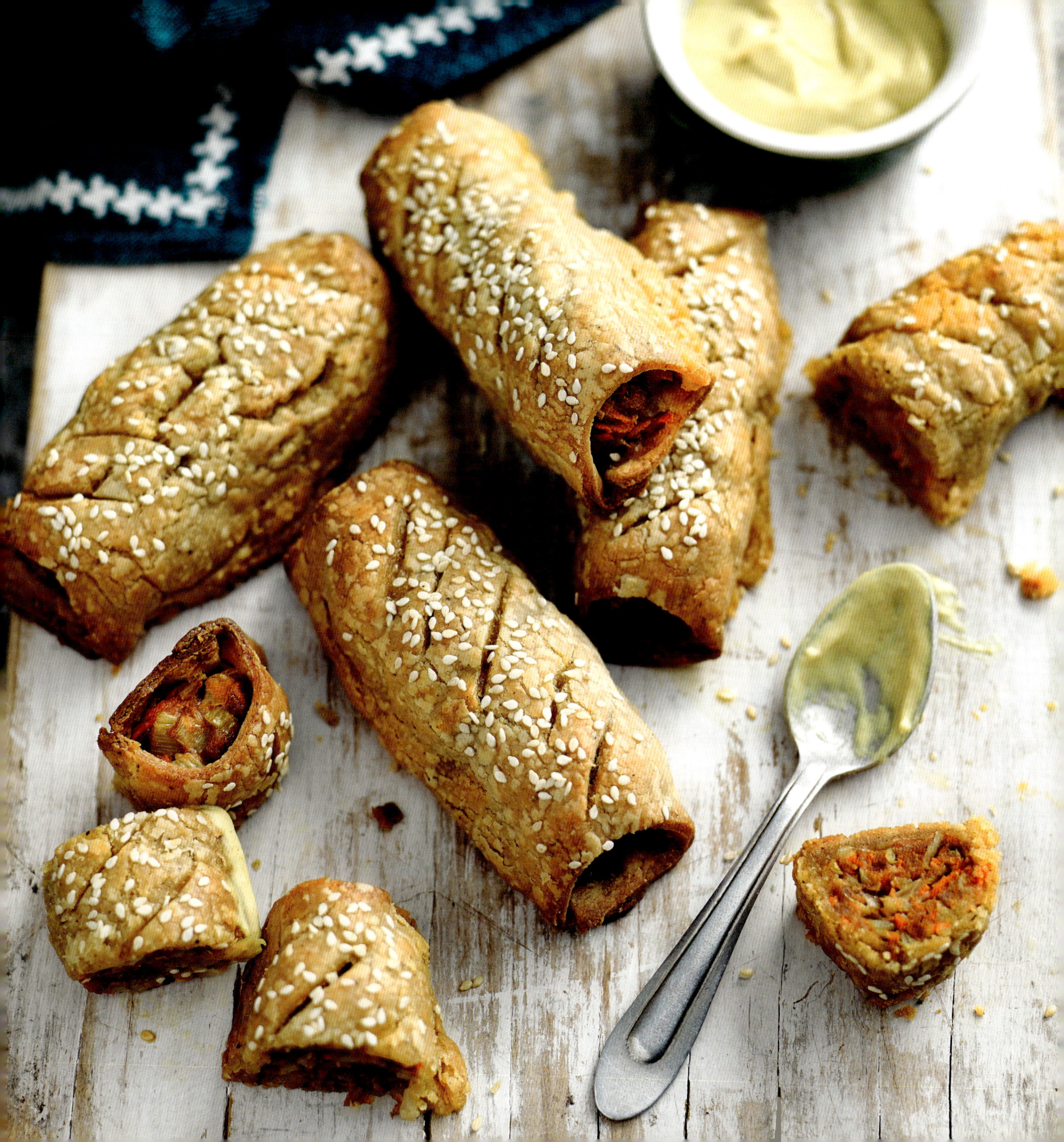

YOU CAN MAKE THIS INTO SIX INDIVIDUAL QUICHES. USE STORE-BOUGHT GLUTEN-FREE SHORTCRUST PASTRY, AVAILABLE FROM MAJOR SUPERMARKETS, IF YOU LIKE.

DINNER

GLUTEN FREE • YEAST FREE • NUT FREE

BACON, CHIVE AND POTATO QUICHE

PREP + COOK TIME 1 HOUR SERVES 6

20g (¾ ounce) butter, melted
1 large potato (300g), chopped coarsely
4 rindless gluten-free bacon slices (260g), chopped coarsely
1 quantity gluten-free pastry (see page 105)
½ cup (60g) coarsely grated tasty cheddar
5 eggs, beaten lightly
½ cup (125ml) milk
2 tablespoons finely chopped fresh chives

1 Preheat oven to 220°C/425°F. Grease a 24cm (9½-inch) round loose-based fluted flan pan with the melted butter.

2 Boil, steam or microwave potato until tender; drain.

3 Cook bacon in a medium frying pan over high heat, stirring, for 5 minutes or until golden. Remove from pan; drain on paper towel.

4 Roll pastry between two sheets of baking paper until 5mm (¼ inch) thick. Ease pastry into pan, pushing together any cracks that might form. Press pastry into side and base of pan; trim edges.

5 Sprinkle bacon, potato and cheddar into pastry case. Whisk eggs, milk and chives in a medium jug, season; pour over bacon mixture.

6 Bake quiche for 30 minutes or until set.

nutritional count per serving 40.9g total fat (20.3g saturated fat); 2874kJ (687 cal); 57.8g carbohydrate; 20.6g protein; 2.1g fibre

seerving suggestion Serve with a mixed green salad.

DINNER

GLUTEN FREE • EGG FREE • YEAST FREE • NUT FREE

FAMILY ROAST CHICKEN AND CORN PIE

PREP + COOK TIME **1 HOUR** SERVES **6**

1 tablespoon olive oil

1 small leek (200g), sliced thinly

500g (1 pound) frozen corn kernels

2 tablespoons 100% corn (maize) cornflour (cornstarch)

2 cups (500ml) gluten-free chicken stock

3 cups coarsely shredded cooked chicken

2 tablespoons coarsely chopped fresh tarragon

1 quantity gluten-free pastry (see page 105)

2 teaspoons sesame seeds

1 Preheat oven to 200°C/400°F.
2 Heat oil in a large frying pan over high heat; cook leek, stirring, for 5 minutes or until softened. Add corn; cook, stirring, for 5 minutes or until hot.
3 Combine cornflour with 2 tablespoons of the stock in a small jug until smooth; stir in remaining stock.
4 Add chicken and stock mixture to corn mixture; cook, stirring occasionally, for 5 minutes or until sauce boils and thickens. Remove from heat. Stir in tarragon; season. Cool slightly.
5 Roll pastry between two sheets of baking paper until 5mm (¼ inch) thick.
6 Spoon chicken mixture into an 2-litre (8-cup) ovenproof dish; top with pastry, trim edges. Brush pastry with a little water, sprinkle with sesame seeds. Make a small cut in the centre of the pastry.
7 Bake pie for 25 minutes or until golden brown and filling is heated through.

nutritional count per serving 33.5g total fat (14.4g saturated fat); 2778kJ (664 cal); 69.1g carbohydrate; 22.1g protein; 4.1g fibre

We used a barbecued chicken. You can use store-bought gluten-free puff pastry, available from major supermarkets; you will need 1 sheet for this recipe. If you don't like the aniseed flavour of tarragon, replace it with coarsely chopped fresh chives or flat-leaf parsley.

YOU CAN USE STORE-BOUGHT GLUTEN-FREE PUFF PASTRY, AVAILABLE FROM MAJOR SUPERMARKETS. THE PIES CAN BE COOKED IN AN ELECTRIC PIE MAKER. FREEZE PIES FOR UP TO 3 MONTHS; REHEAT FROM FROZEN IN A 180°C/350°F OVEN FOR 30 MINUTES OR UNTIL PIES ARE HEATED THROUGH.

DINNER

GLUTEN FREE • DAIRY FREE • EGG FREE • YEAST FREE • NUT FREE

BEEF PIES

PREP + COOK TIME 2½ HOURS (+ COOLING & REFRIGERATION)   MAKES 6

1 tablespoon olive oil

800g (1½ pounds) gravy beef, cut into 2cm (¾-inch) pieces

2 medium brown onions (300g), chopped finely

1 clove garlic, crushed

2 tablespoons tomato paste

1 tablespoon dijon mustard

2½ cups (625ml) gluten-free beef stock

2 tablespoons 100% corn (maize) cornflour (cornstarch)

2 tablespoons water

1 quantity gluten-free pastry (see page 105)

1 Heat oil in a medium saucepan over high heat; cook beef, in batches, stirring, for 2 minutes or until browned. Remove from pan.

2 Reduce heat to medium; cook onion and garlic in same pan, stirring, for 5 minutes or until onion is softened. Return beef to pan with combined paste, mustard and beef stock; bring to the boil. Reduce heat to low; simmer, uncovered, stirring, occasionally, for 1½ hours or until beef is tender and sauce thickens.

3 Combine cornflour and the water; add to beef mixture. Cook, stirring, over high heat, for 5 minutes or until sauce boils and thickens. Season to taste. Cool.

4 Preheat oven to 220°C/425°F. Oil six 10cm (4-inch), ¾ cup (180ml) pie dishes. Place dishes on an oven tray.

5 Roll pastry between two sheets of baking paper until 5mm (¼ inch) thick. Cut six 15cm (6-inch) rounds from pastry. Ease pastry rounds into dishes; press into base and sides; trim edges.

6 Spoon beef mixture into pastry cases. Brush edges with water. Cut six 10cm (5¼-inch) rounds from remaining pastry; place on pies, press to seal, trim edges. Refrigerate 30 minutes.

7 Make two small cuts into the top of each pie. Bake for 30 minutes or until tops are firm, browned lightly and filling is hot.

nutritional count per pie 34.3g total fat (14.5g saturated fat); 2673kJ (638 cal); 50.5g carbohydrate; 33.7g protein; 2.4g fibre

serving suggestion Serve with peas and gluten-free oven-baked chips.

DINNER

GLUTEN FREE • DAIRY FREE • EGG FREE • NUT FREE
MEDITERRANEAN MEATLOAF

PREP + COOK TIME **1 HOUR** SERVES **8**

8 thin slices prosciutto (120g)

750g (1½ pounds) minced (ground) beef

1 small brown onion (80g), grated coarsely

2 cups (140g) stale gluten-free breadcrumbs

½ cup (75g) sun-dried tomatoes in oil, drained, sliced thinly

4 slices bottled roasted red capsicum (170g), drained, sliced thinly

¼ cup (40g) pitted black olives

¼ cup (35g) pimento-stuffed green olives

¼ cup loosely packed fresh oregano leaves

1 Preheat oven to 180°C/350°F. Oil a 10cm x 21cm (4-inch x 8½-inch) loaf pan. Arrange 6 slices of the prosciutto over base and long sides of the pan.
2 Combine beef, onion and breadcrumbs in a large bowl. Add tomato, capsicum, olives and oregano; combine mixture using your hands. Season.
3 Press beef mixture into pan; cover with remaining prosciutto slices, cutting the slices to fit. Place pan on an oven tray.
4 Bake meatloaf for 50 minutes or until golden brown and cooked through.

nutritional count per serving 16.9g total fat (6.8g saturated fat); 1437kJ (343 cal); 15.6g carbohydrate; 30.8g protein; 2.7g fibre

tips The meatloaf can be prepared a day ahead; store, covered, in the fridge. If you like, swap the beef mince for chicken mince. Add a tablespoon of tomato paste for extra tomato flavour.

serving suggestion Serve with roasted vegetables or a green leafy salad.

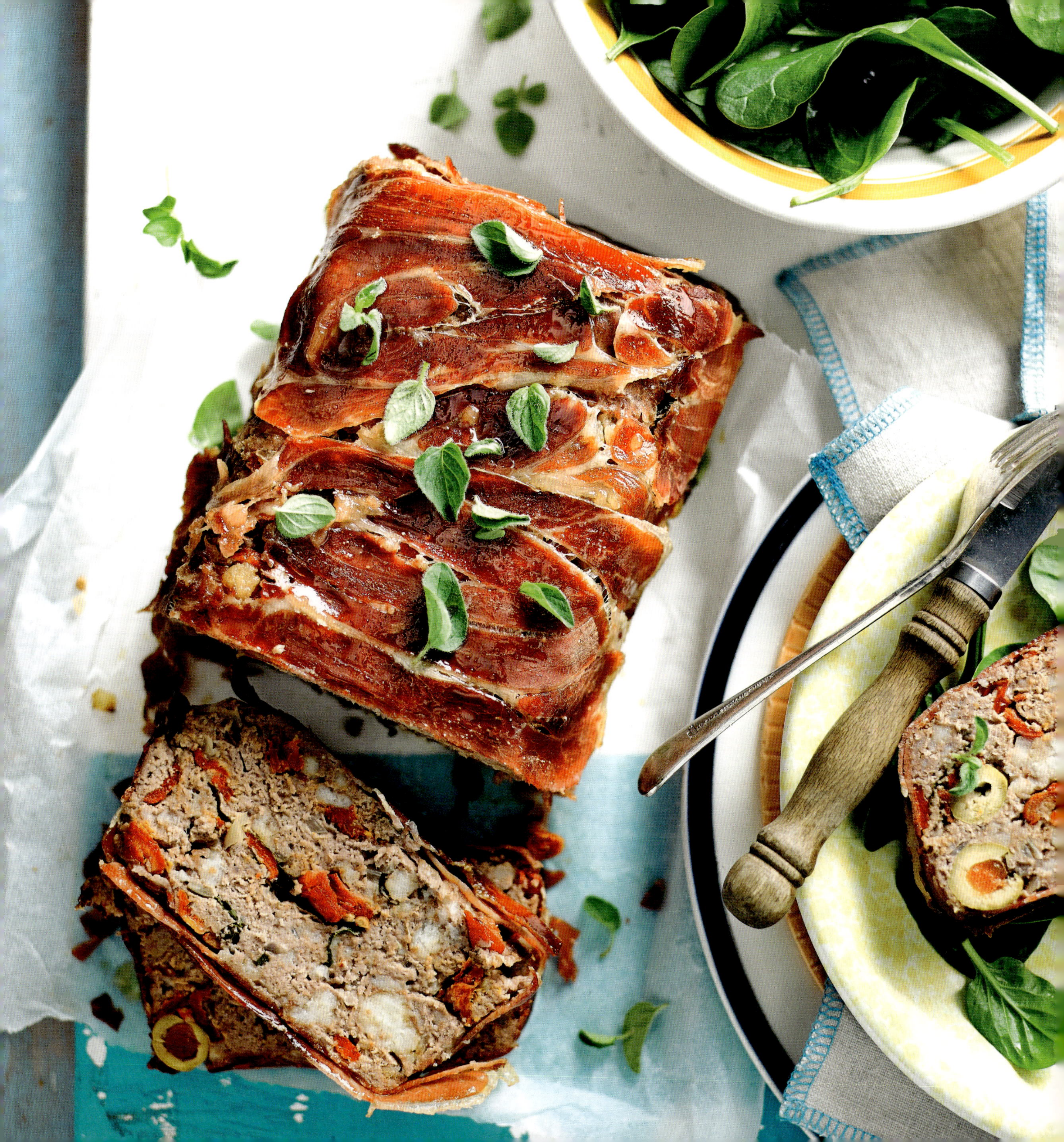

DIVIDE THE DOUGH INTO 6 EQUAL PORTIONS TO MAKE MINI PIZZAS. TO FREEZE PIZZA BASES, PAR-BAKE PIZZA DOUGH FOR 15 MINUTES OR UNTIL BROWNED LIGHTLY, THEN COOL. WRAP INDIVIDUALLY IN PLASTIC WRAP, THEN FOIL. FREEZE FOR UP TO 3 MONTHS.

DINNER

GLUTEN FREE • DAIRY FREE • NUT FREE

GLUTEN-FREE PIZZA DOUGH

PREP TIME 30 MINUTES (+ STANDING) MAKES 3 BASES

3 cups (405g) gluten-free plain (all-purpose) flour

1 cup (135g) gluten-free self-raising flour

½ cup (75g) potato flour

½ cup (80g) brown rice flour

½ cup (90g) white rice flour

2 teaspoons (7g) dried yeast

2 teaspoons xantham gum

2 teaspoons salt

1 egg

3 egg whites

¾ cup (180ml) olive oil

1 teaspoon white vinegar

2 cups (500ml) warm water, approximately

white rice flour, extra, for dusting

1 Grease three 30cm (12-inch) round pizza trays, dust lightly with a little rice flour.
2 Combine dry ingredients in a large bowl.
3 Beat egg, egg whites, oil, vinegar and 1½ cups of the water in a large bowl of an electric mixer on medium speed for 3½ minutes. Add the combined sifted dry ingredients, 1 cup at a time, beating until combined between additions. Continue adding dry ingredients until mixture just starts to come away from the side of the bowl (add remaining water only if necessary). Turn dough onto a surface dusted with rice flour; knead lightly until smooth.
4 Divide dough into three equal portions. Roll each portion on the rice-floured surface until large enough to fit pizza trays. Lift dough onto trays. Cover; stand in a warm place for 45 minutes.
5 Spread pizza dough with sauces and toppings as desired. For pizza topping suggestions, see recipes on pages 118, 121, 122 & 125).

nutritional count per serving 58.5g total fat (8.6g saturated fat); 6090kJ (1455 cal); 216.3g carbohydrate; 12.6g protein; 3g fibre

DINNER

GLUTEN FREE • NUT FREE

ROASTED VEGETABLES AND BOCCONCINI PIZZA

PREP + COOK TIME 50 MINUTES   SERVES 4

- rice flour, for dusting
- ⅓ quantity gluten-free pizza dough (see page 117)
- 200g (6½ ounces) pumpkin, cut into 1cm (½-inch) cubes
- 1 medium zucchini (120g), sliced thinly
- 1 small red capsicum (150g), quartered
- 1 small eggplant (230g), sliced thinly
- ¼ cup (65g) tomato pasta sauce
- 1 cup (100g) pizza cheese
- 100g (3 ounces) baby bocconcini
- 40g (1½ ounces) rocket (arugula) leaves

1 Preheat oven to 220°C/425°F.

2 Oil a 30cm (12-inch) round pizza pan, then dust with rice flour. Roll pizza dough on a surface dusted with rice flour into a 30cm (12-inch) round; place on tray. Cover; stand until needed.

3 Place pumpkin on an oiled baking tray; roast for 20 minutes or until tender and cubes are browned around the edges.

4 Meanwhile, cook zucchini, capsicum and eggplant on a heated oiled grill pan (or grill or barbecue) until browned lightly and tender. Season to taste.

5 Spread pizza base with sauce; top with pizza cheese, vegetables and bocconcini.

6 Bake pizza for 15 minutes or until cheese is golden and base is crisp. Just before serving, top with rocket.

nutritional count per serving 26.1g total fat (9.2g saturated fat); 2372kJ (567 cal); 61.4g carbohydrate; 19.2g protein; 4.2g fibre

tips You can use a store-bought gluten-free pizza base instead, if you prefer. If the pizza base is not crisping as much as you would like, place the cooked pizza on an oiled, heated grill pan (or barbecue plate) for a few minutes.

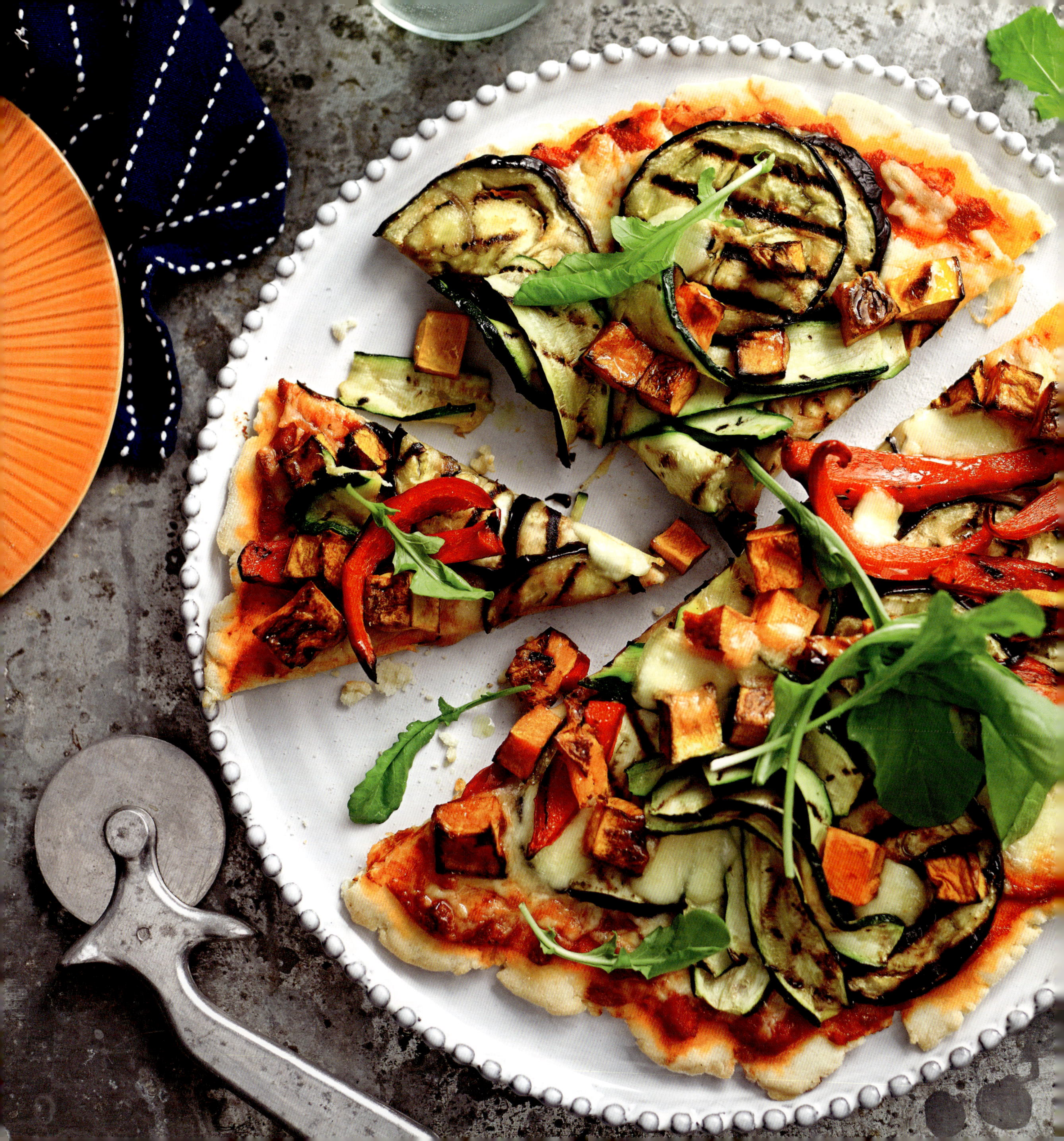

USE A STORE-BOUGHT GLUTEN-FREE PIZZA BASE, IF YOU PREFER.

IF THE PIZZA BASE IS NOT CRISPING AS MUCH AS YOU WOULD LIKE,

PLACE THE COOKED PIZZA ON AN OILED, HEATED GRILL PAN

(OR BARBECUE PLATE) FOR A FEW MINUTES.

DINNER

GLUTEN FREE • NUT FREE
PUTTENESCA PIZZA

PREP + COOK TIME 45 MINUTES SERVES 4

rice flour, for dusting

⅓ quantity gluten-free pizza dough (see page 117)

250g (8 ounces) baby roma (egg) tomatoes

1 teaspoon olive oil

200g (6½ ounces) canned diced tomatoes

4 anchovy fillets, chopped finely

1 tablespoon fresh rosemary sprigs

1 cup (100g) pizza cheese

100g (3 ounces) thinly sliced gluten-free danish salami

¼ cup (40g) mixed pitted olives, sliced thinly

¼ teaspoon dried chilli flakes

rosemary sprigs, extra, to serve

oregano leaves, to serve (optional)

1 Preheat oven to 220°C/450°F.

2 Oil a 30cm (12-inch) round pizza tray, then dust with rice flour. Roll dough on a surface dusted with rice flour into a 30cm (12-inch) round; place on tray. Cover; stand until needed.

3 Place roma tomatoes on a baking tray; drizzle with oil, season. Roast for 10 minutes or until just softened.

4 Meanwhile, place canned tomatoes, anchovy and rosemary in a medium frying pan over high heat; cook, stirring, for 5 minutes or until thickened slightly. Season to taste.

5 Spread pizza base with tomato mixture; top with pizza cheese, roasted tomatoes, salami, olives and chilli flakes.

6 Bake pizza for 20 minutes or until golden brown and cheese melts. Just before serving, top with extra rosemary and oregano.

nutritional count per serving 31.7g total fat (9.3g saturated fat); 2509kJ (599 cal); 59.5g carbohydrate; 17.3g protein; 1.8g fibre

serving suggestion Serve with a mixed salad of baby rocket (arugula) leaves, semi-dried tomato and shaved parmesan.

DINNER

GLUTEN FREE • NUT FREE

CARAMELISED ONION AND SPICY SAUSAGE PIZZA

PREP + COOK TIME 1 HOUR SERVES 4

rice flour, for dusting
⅓ quantity gluten-free pizza dough (see page 117)
1 tablespoon olive oil
2 large red onions (600g), sliced thickly
2 cloves garlic, crushed
2 teaspoons fresh thyme leaves
1 tablespoon caster (superfine) sugar
1 tablespoon red wine vinegar
375g (12 ounces) extra lean gluten-free italian-style sausages, casings removed
1 cup (100g) pizza cheese
40g (1½ ounces) baby rocket (arugula) leaves

1 Preheat oven to 220°C/425°F.
2 Oil a 30cm (12-inch) round pizza pan; dust with rice flour. Roll pizza dough on a surface dusted with rice flour into a 30cm (12-inch) round; place on tray. Cover; stand until needed.
3 Heat oil in a large frying pan over low heat; cook onion, stirring occasionally, for 15 minutes or until onion softens and is browned lightly. Add garlic and thyme; cook for 2 minutes or until fragrant. Increase heat to high, add sugar and vinegar; cook, stirring, for 5 minutes or until sugar dissolves and mixture thickens slightly. Season to taste.
4 Meanwhile, heat a large non-stick frying pan over high heat. Break sausage meat into small balls, add to pan; cook, turning, for 3 minutes or until browned all over.
5 Sprinkle pizza base with half the pizza cheese; top with the onion and sausage, sprinkle with remaining pizza cheese.
6 Bake pizza for 20 minutes or until golden brown. Just before serving, top with rocket.

nutritional count per serving 39.5g total fat (12.8g saturated fat); 2948kJ (704 cal); 65.4g carbohydrate; 19.9g protein; 4.6g fibre

tips For darker caramelised onions, use brown onions with brown sugar and balsamic vinegar. You can use a store-bought gluten-free pizza base instead, if you prefer. If the pizza base is not crisping as much as you would like, place the cooked pizza on an oiled, heated grill pan (or barbecue plate) for a few minutes.

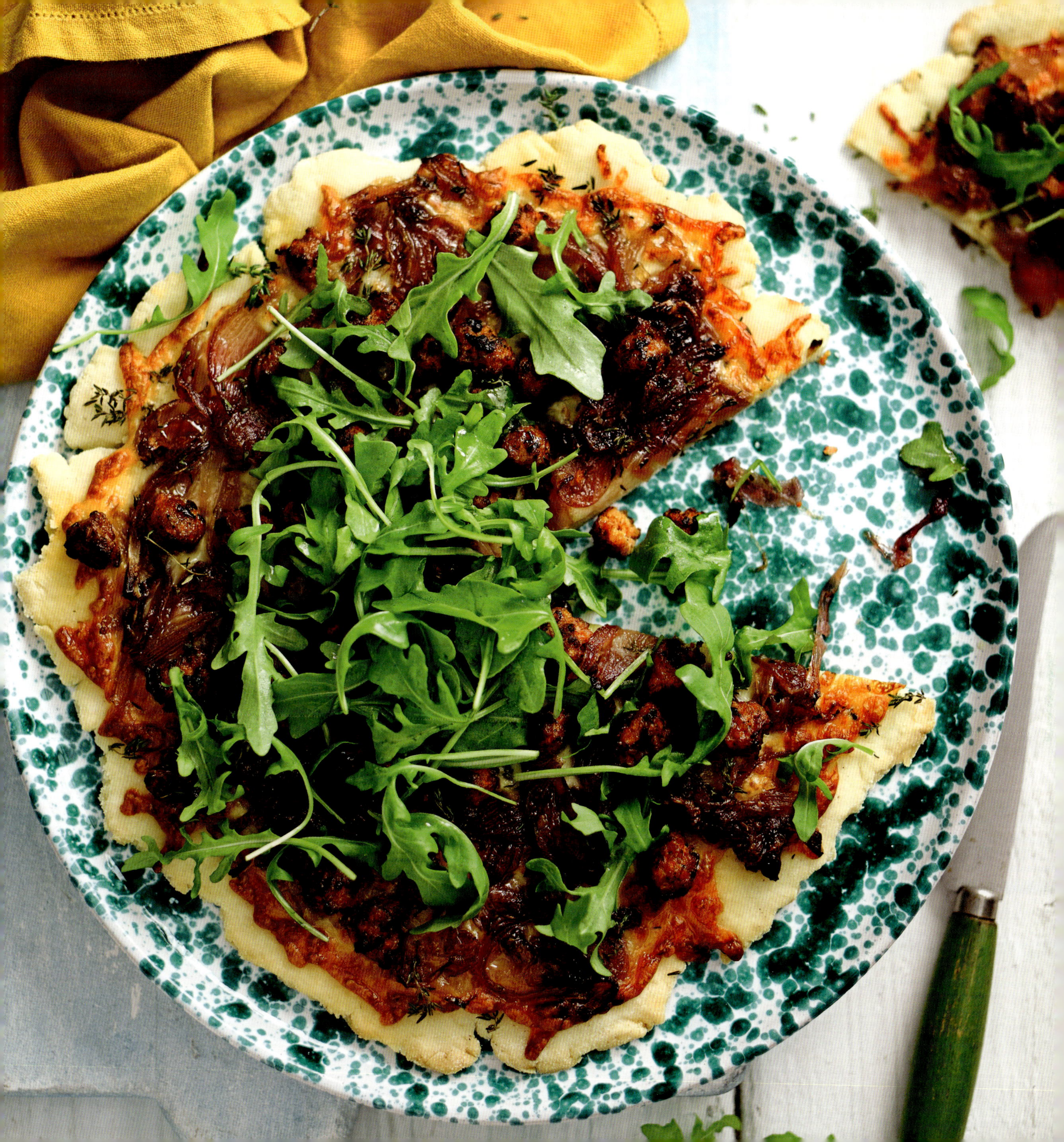

You can use a store-bought gluten-free pizza base instead, if you prefer. Swap lamb for beef or chicken mince. If the pizza base is not crisping as much as you would like, place the cooked pizzas on an oiled, heated grill pan (or barbecue plate) for a few minutes.

GLUTEN FREE • NUT FREE

SPICY LAMB, SPINACH AND FETTA PIZZAS

PREP + COOK TIME 45 MINUTES **MAKES** 4

rice flour, for dusting

⅓ quantity gluten-free pizza dough (see page 117)

1 tablespoon olive oil

250g (8 ounces) minced (ground) lamb

½ teaspoon ground cumin

½ teaspoon ground coriander

½ teaspoon ground cinnamon

½ teaspoon ground paprika

1 cup (100g) pizza cheese

60g (2 ounces) baby spinach leaves

100g (3 ounces) fetta, crumbled

2 tablespoons gluten-free plain yoghurt

lemon wedges, to serve

1 Preheat oven to 200°C/400°F.

2 Oil two oven trays, then dust with rice flour. Divide pizza dough into four portions. Roll each portion on a surface dusted with rice flour into 15cm (6-inch) rounds; place on trays. Cover; stand until needed.

3 Heat oil in a large frying pan over high heat, add lamb; cook, stirring, until lamb changes colour. Add spices; cook, stirring, for 2 minutes or until fragrant. Remove from heat. Cool slightly.

4 Sprinkle pizza cheese over pizza bases; top with half the spinach, then all the lamb mixture and fetta.

5 Bake pizzas for 20 minutes or until golden and cheese is melted. Just before serving, top with remaining spinach and yoghurt; squeeze with lemon.

nutritional count per pizza 36.2g total fat (13.3g saturated fat); 2793kJ (667 cal); 55g carbohydrate; 29.2g protein; 1.4g fibre

GLUTEN FREE • DAIRY FREE • NUT FREE

BEEF AND RICE STIR-FRY WITH CARROT AND CUCUMBER PICKLE

PREP + COOK TIME 20 MINUTES SERVES 4

500g (1-pound) packet microwave brown rice

2 tablespoons olive oil

4 eggs, beaten lightly

1 clove garlic, crushed

1 tablespoon grated fresh ginger

400g (12½ ounces) lean minced (ground) beef

1 tablespoon gluten-free oyster sauce

4 cups (320g) shredded cabbage

⅓ cup shredded fresh mint leaves

2 green onions (scallions), sliced thinly

CARROT AND CUCUMBER PICKLE

⅔ cup (160ml) rice wine vinegar

⅓ cup (75g) caster (superfine) sugar

¼ teaspoon dried chilli flakes

1 medium carrot (120g), cut into matchsticks

2 lebanese cucumbers (260g), seeded, cut into matchsticks

1 Cook rice according to packet instructions.

2 Make carrot and cucumber pickle.

3 Heat 1 teaspoon of the oil in a wok over high heat; add a quarter of the egg, swirl wok to make a thin omelette. Cook, uncovered, until egg is just set. Remove from wok; roll tightly, cut into thick strips. Repeat using 3 teaspoons of the oil and remaining egg to make three more omelettes. Roll tightly; cut into thick strips.

4 Heat remaining oil in wok over high heat; stir-fry garlic and ginger until fragrant. Add beef; cook, stirring, until beef is browned. Add sauce; stir-fry until heated through. Remove from wok.

5 Stir-fry cabbage in wok (add a little water if needed) until tender. Return beef to wok with rice and mint; stir-fry until hot.

6 Drain carrot and cucumber pickle; serve rice topped with pickle, omelette and onion.

CARROT AND CUCUMBER PICKLE Combine vinegar, sugar and chilli flakes in a small bowl until sugar dissolves. Add carrot and cucumber; toss to combine.

nutritional count per serving 21.8g total fat (6.1g saturated fat); 2339kJ (559 cal); 51.5g carbohydrate; 35.5g protein; 6.7g fibre

Omit the rice and serve the beef and pickle mixtures in lettuce leaves, if you like. To cook your own brown rice you will need to boil ¾ cup (150g) brown rice in water for 25 minutes or until tender; drain well.

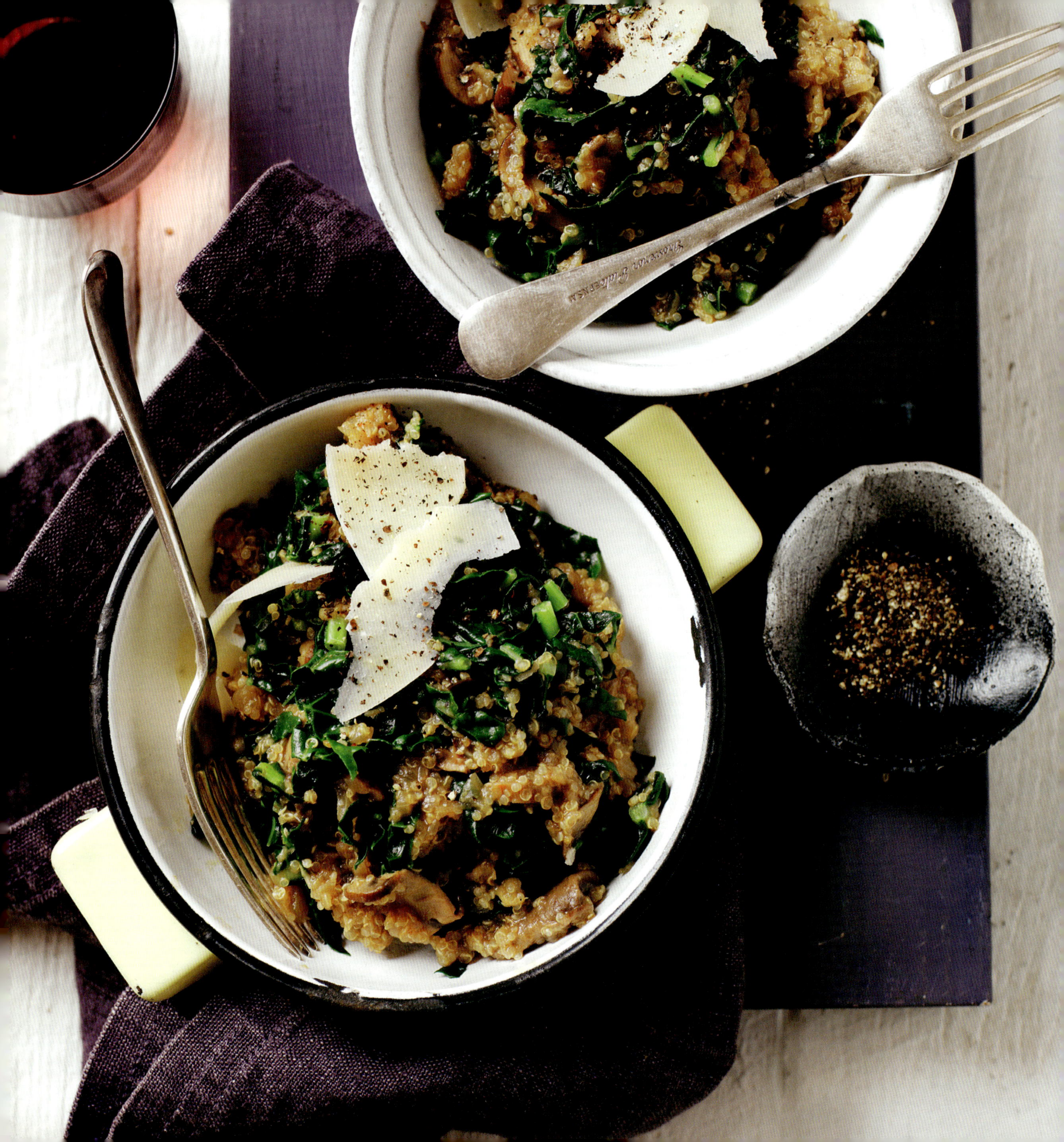

DINNER

GLUTEN FREE • EGG FREE • NUT FREE

MUSHROOM, CAVOLO NERO AND QUINOA RISOTTO

PREP + COOK TIME 40 MINUTES SERVES 4

20g (¾ ounce) dried porcini mushrooms

½ cup (125ml) boiling water

1 tablespoon olive oil

1 medium brown onion (150g), chopped finely

2 flat mushroom (160g), chopped coarsely

200g (6½ ounces) swiss brown mushrooms, sliced thinly

2 cloves garlic, crushed

1 cup quinoa (200g), rinsed, drained

1.25 litres (5 cups) gluten-free vegetable stock

2 sprig fresh thyme

200g (6½ ounces) cavolo nero, sliced thinly

⅔ cup (50g) finely grated parmesan

1 Place porcini mushrooms in a heatproof bowl; cover with the boiling water. Stand for 5 minutes.
2 Meanwhile, heat oil in a medium frying pan over medium heat; cook onion, stirring, for 3 minutes or until soft. Add flat and swiss brown mushrooms; cook, stirring, for 3 minutes or until browned and tender. Add garlic; cook, stirring, for 1 minute or until fragrant.
3 Stir in quinoa, stock and thyme. Remove porcini mushrooms from water (reserve the soaking liquid); chop coarsely. Add porcini mushrooms and soaking liquid to pan. Bring to the boil; simmer, uncovered for 20 minutes until liquid is absorbed and quinoa is tender. Discard thyme.
4 Add cavolo nero; stir until wilted. Remove from heat; stir through half the parmesan.
5 Serve risotto topped with remaining parmesan.

nutritional count per serving 16.9g total fat (4.3g saturated fat); 1743kJ (416 cal); 41g carbohydrate; 19.7g protein; 10.7g fibre

tip Cavolo nero is also known as tuscan cabbage; it is highly nutritious, and is also great to use in soups, salads and stir-fries.

DINNER

GLUTEN FREE • DAIRY FREE • EGG FREE • NUT FREE

JERK SALMON WITH BLACK BEAN SALAD

PREP + COOK TIME 25 MINUTES   SERVES 4

2 teaspoons ground coriander

1 teaspoon dried thyme

½ teaspoon ground cinnamon

½ teaspoon chilli powder

½ teaspoon ground allspice

1 clove garlic, crushed

4 x 100g (3-ounce) salmon fillets, skin and bones removed

2 trimmed corn cobs (500g)

cooking-oil spray

1 cup (200g) canned black beans, drained, rinsed

200g (6½ ounces) cherry tomatoes, halved

1 small avocado (200g), chopped coarsely

1 green onion (scallion), sliced thinly

1 cup loosely packed fresh coriander (cilantro) leaves

1 tablespoon olive oil

1 tablespoon lime juice

1 Combine ground coriander, dried thyme, cinnamon, chilli powder, allspice and garlic in a small bowl; rub all over salmon.
2 Meanwhile, cook corn in a medium saucepan of boiling water for 6 minutes or until tender; drain. Cool.
3 Spray a large non-stick frying pan with oil; cook salmon, over medium heat, for 3 minutes each side or until just cooked.
4 Meanwhile, cut kernels from corn. Place kernels in a large bowl with beans, tomato, avocado, green onion, fresh coriander and combined oil and juice; toss gently to combine.
5 Serve salmon with salad and, if you like, lime wedges.

nutritional count per serving 22.3g total fat (4.6g saturated fat); 1819kJ (434 cal); 27g carbohydrate; 25.5g protein; 13g fibre

ADD MORE CHILLI POWDER TO THE SPICE MIX IF YOU LIKE IT HOT.
BLACK BEANS ARE AVAILABLE FROM SPECIALTY FOOD STORES.
YOU CAN SUBSTITUTE KIDNEY OR CANNELLINI BEANS, IF YOU LIKE.

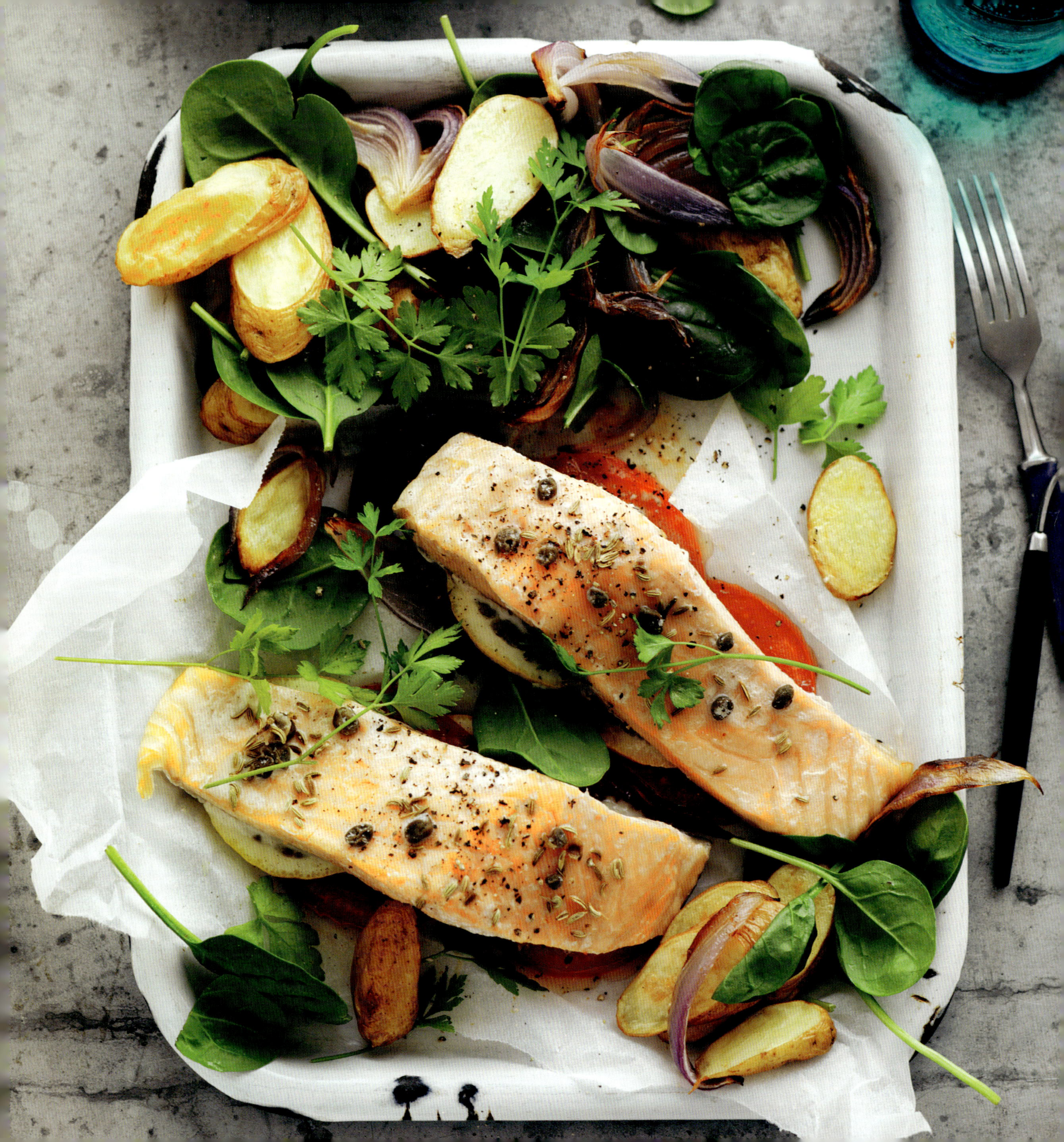

GLUTEN FREE • DAIRY FREE • EGG FREE • NUT FREE

SALMON PARCELS WITH KIPFLER POTATOES

PREP + COOK TIME 50 MINUTES SERVES 4

600g (1¼ pounds) kipfler (fingerling) potatoes, sliced thinly

1 medium red onion (170g), cut into wedges

1 tablespoon olive oil

1 lemon (140g), sliced thinly

2 small tomato (180g), sliced thinly

4 x 150g (9½-ounce) salmon fillets, skin and bones removed

1 tablespoon drained baby capers, rinsed

2 teaspoons fennel seeds

150g (4½ ounces) baby spinach leaves

½ cup firmly packed fresh parsley leaves

1 Preheat oven to 200°C/400°F.
2 Combine potatoes and onion in a medium baking dish; drizzle with half the oil. Roast for 30 minutes or until browned lightly and tender.
3 Meanwhile, arrange lemon and tomato slices on two 30cm (12-inch) squares of baking paper; top with salmon, capers and seeds, drizzle with remaining oil. Fold paper into a parcel to enclose salmon; place on a baking tray. Bake for 8 minutes or until salmon is cooked as you like.
4 Toss spinach through potato mixture.
5 Serve fish with potato mixture, topped with parsley.

nutritional count per serving 15.6g total fat (3.1g saturated fat); 1642kJ (392 cal); 23.2g carbohydrate; 35.5g protein; 5g fibre

tips Baking the salmon in a parcel means all the flavours, juices and steam are locked in to give a moist and tasty end result. You could try this recipe with firm white fish fillets or even chicken breast. The cooking time will vary depending on the thickness of the cut.

SWEET

BEFORE YOU START BASIC STEPS

MELTING CHOCOLATE
Place roughly chopped chocolate into a heatproof bowl over a saucepan of barely simmering water. The water mustn't touch the base of the bowl. Stir chocolate until smooth, and remove from the pan as soon as it's melted.

MAKING SCONES
Turn the scone dough onto a lightly gluten-free floured surface; pat out into a 3cm (1¼-inch) thickness. Cut out 5cm (2-inch) rounds. Place scones, just touching, on tray. Gently knead scraps of dough together; repeat process.

SWEET

GREASING A BABA PAN
A baba pan has a pretty fluted base, which becomes the top of the cake. Grease the pan with softened butter and a pastry brush to coat the base, side and all the edges. Sprinkle the pan with rice flour then tap out the excess.

ZESTING CITRUS FRUIT
A zesting tool has very small, and very sharp, holes that cut the rind into thin ribbons or strips, but leaves the bitter pith behind. Press the holes of the zester firmly onto the rind, pulling it down the fruit.

SWEET

GLUTEN FREE • YEAST FREE • NUT FREE

LEMONTONS

PREP + COOK TIME 1 HOUR (+ STANDING) MAKES 16

4 eggs

⅔ cup (150g) caster (superfine) sugar

⅓ cup (50g) 100% corn (maize) cornflour (cornstarch)

⅓ cup (45g) gluten-free self-raising flour

⅓ cup (45g) gluten-free plain (all-purpose) flour

1 cup (250ml) store-bought gluten-free lemon curd

1½ cups (240g) gluten-free icing sugar (pure confectioners' sugar)

⅓ cup (80ml) lemon juice

½ cup (125ml) boiling water

3 cups (300g) shredded coconut

1 Preheat oven to 180°C/350°F. Grease a deep 23cm (9-inch) square cake pan; line base with baking paper.
2 Beat eggs and caster sugar in a large bowl with an electric mixer for 8 minutes or until mixture is thick and creamy.
3 Triple sift flours. Whisk flour mixture into egg mixture until just combined. Pour mixture into pan.
4 Bake cake for 25 minutes or until cake is dry to the touch and edges are coming away from the sides of the pan. Stand cake in pan for 5 minutes before turning, top-side up, onto a wire rack to cool completely.
5 Combine lemon curd, sifted icing sugar, juice and the water in a large bowl until well combined. Place coconut on a large plate.
6 Cut cake into 16 squares. Use two forks to dip squares, one at a time, into lemon mixture until coated all over; toss in coconut. Place on a wire rack until firm.

nutritional count per lemonton 16.5g total fat (11.1g saturated fat); 1239kJ (296 cal); 41.8g carbohydrate; 3.6g protein; 2.9g fibre

tips Lemontons can be made a day ahead; store in an airtight container. Make strawberry lamingtons by dipping the sponge into gluten-free strawberry topping and coating in coconut tinted with pink food colouring.

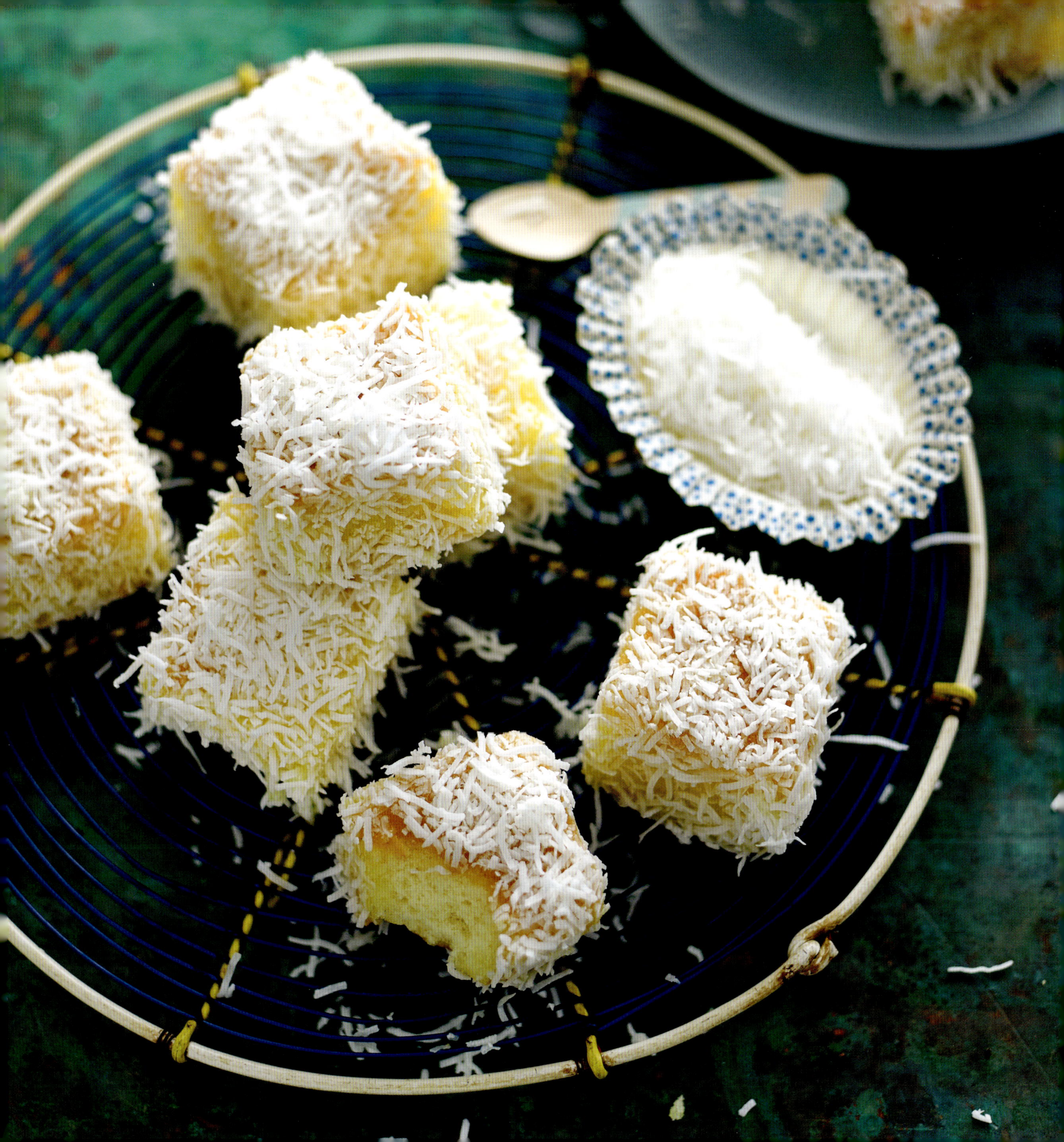

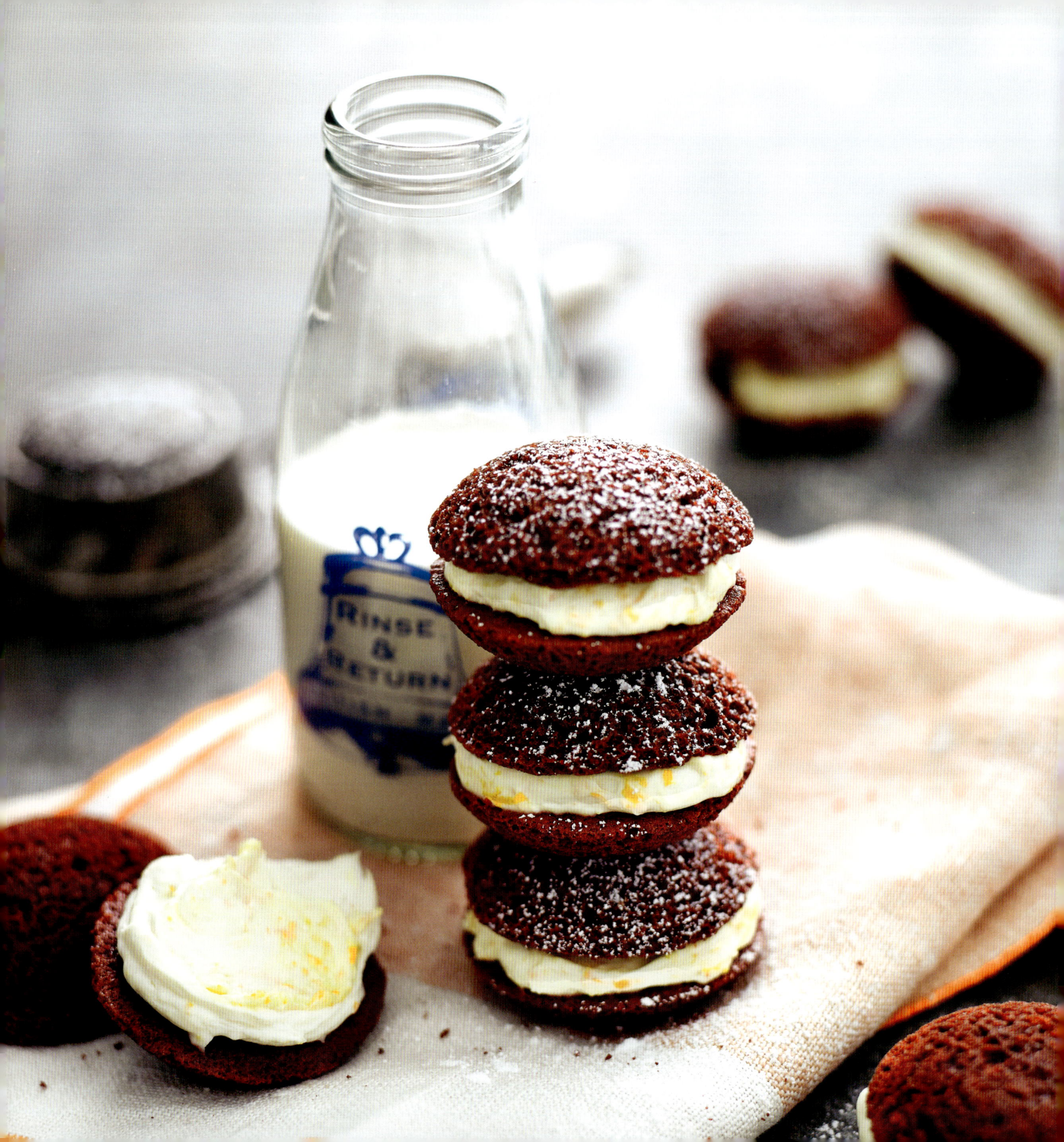
RINSE
&
RETURN

SWEET

GLUTEN FREE • DAIRY FREE • YEAST FREE • NUT FREE

RED VELVET WHOOPIE PIES WITH ORANGE FILLING

PREP + COOK TIME 30 MINUTES (+ COOLING) MAKES 12

dairy-free spread, for greasing

75g (2½ ounces) dairy-free spread

⅓ cup (75g) caster (superfine) sugar

1 egg

¾ cup (100g) gluten-free self-raising flour

1 tablespoon baby rice cereal (farex)

1 tablespoon cocoa powder

¼ cup (60ml) soy milk

1 teaspoon red food colouring

½ cup (120g) tofutti better than cream cheese, softened (see tips)

1 tablespoon caster (superfine) sugar, extra

1 teaspoon finely grated orange rind

1 tablespoon gluten-free icing sugar (pure confectioners' sugar)

1 Preheat oven to 160°C/325°F. Grease two 12-hole (1 tablespoon/20ml) shallow round-based patty pans with dairy-free spread.
2 Beat dairy-free spread and sugar in a medium bowl with an electric mixer until combined. Beat in egg until combined. Stir in the sifted flour, rice cereal and cocoa, and milk, alternately, stirring after each addition. Stir in colouring. Drop rounded teaspoons of mixture into pan holes; smooth tops.
3 Bake cakes for 8 minutes or until cooked through. Transfer to a wire rack to cool.
4 Combine tofutti, extra sugar and rind in a small bowl. Sandwich cakes with filling. Just before serving, dust whoopie pies with sifted icing sugar.

nutritional count per whoopie pie 8g total fat (2g saturated fat); 575kJ (137 cal); 14.4g carbohydrate; 2.1g protein; 0.5g fibre

tips 'Tofutti better than cream cheese' is a tofu-based dairy-free cream cheese substitute, available in the refrigerated section of health food stores and major supermarkets. If you are not dairy intolerant, you can replace the dairy-free spread with butter and the tofutti with cream cheese.

SWEET

GLUTEN FREE • DAIRY FREE • YEAST FREE • NUT FREE

DARK CHOCOLATE CHEESECAKE BROWNIE

PREP + COOK TIME 1¾ HOURS (+ COOLING) MAKES 24

dairy-free spread, for greasing
150g (4½ ounces) dairy-free dark chocolate, chopped coarsely
150g (4½ ounces) dairy-free spread
1¼ cups (275g) caster (superfine) sugar
2 eggs, beaten lightly
2 teaspoons vanilla extract
½ cup (65g) gluten-free self-raising flour
½ cup (75g) tapioca flour
⅓ cup (35g) dutch-processed cocoa
227g (7 ounces) tofutti better than cream cheese, softened (see tips)
1 tablespoon caster (superfine) sugar, extra

1 Preheat oven to 160°C/325°F. Grease a deep 22cm (9-inch) square cake pan with dairy-free spread; line base and sides with baking paper.
2 Stir chocolate and dairy-free spread in a medium saucepan over low heat for 5 minutes or until chocolate melts and mixture is smooth. Remove from heat. Cool for 5 minutes.
3 Stir sugar into chocolate mixture; add eggs and half the extract, stir to combine. Stir in sifted flours and cocoa until combined. Pour mixture into pan.
4 Combine tofutti, extra sugar and remaining extract in a small bowl. Drop large spoonfuls of tofutti mixture over chocolate mixture. Use a knife to gently swirl the mixtures together to create a marble effect.
5 Bake brownie for 1¼ hours or until a skewer inserted in the centre comes out clean. Cool brownie in pan before cutting into 24 squares.

nutritional count per piece 10g total fat (3.3g saturated fat); 755kJ (180 cal); 21.5g carbohydrate; 1.5g protein; 0.4g fibre

tips 'Tofutti better than cream cheese' is a tofu-based dairy-free cream cheese substitute, available in the refrigerated section of health food stores and major supermarkets. If you are not dairy intolerant, you can replace the dairy-free spread with butter, dairy-free dark chocolate with dark chcocolate, and the tofutti with cream cheese.

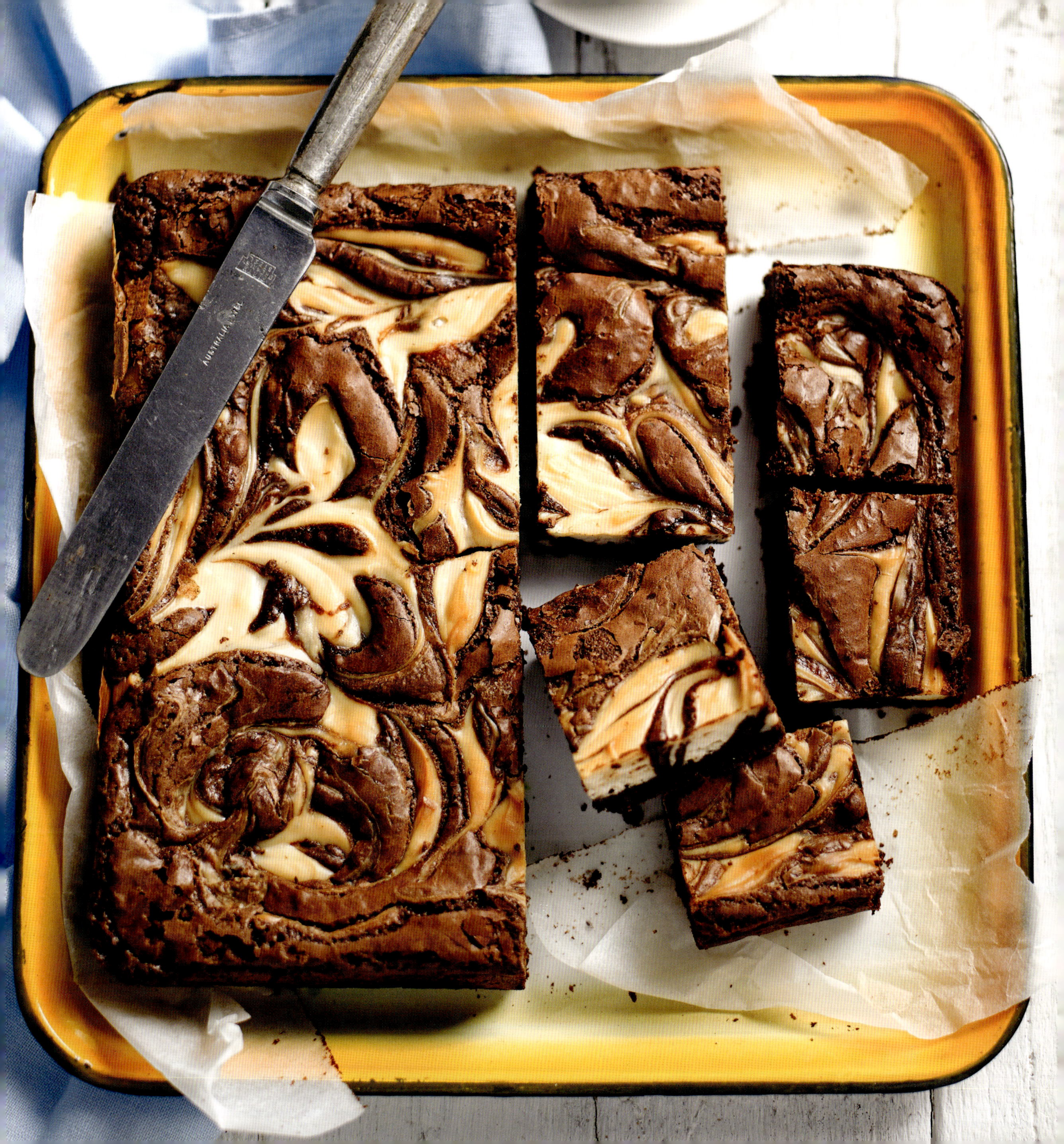

YOU WILL NEED A 1 KG (2-POUND) CONTAINER OF PEACH SLICES IN NATURAL JUICE FOR THIS RECIPE. YOU COULD ALSO TRY THIS WITH OTHER CANNED FRUITS SUCH AS PLUM OR MANGO.

SWEET

GLUTEN FREE • EGG FREE • NUT FREE

FROZEN PEACH LASSI

PREP TIME 10 MINUTES (+ FREEZING) SERVES 4

Lassi is a yoghurt-based drink from India. Our frozen version here transforms it into a cooling dessert.

2 cups (365g) drained canned peach slices in natural juice

1 cup (280g) low-fat gluten-free plain yoghurt

½ cup (125ml) buttermilk

2 tablespoons honey

2 teaspoons finely grated lime rind

2 teaspoons lime juice

1 cup (180g) drained canned peach slices in natural juice, extra

1 teaspoon finely grated lime rind, extra

1 Blend or process peaches until smooth.
2 Whisk peach puree with yoghurt, buttermilk, honey, rind and juice in a large bowl.
3 Pour mixture into a 1 litre (4-cup) container. Cover tightly with foil; freeze for 3 hours or overnight
4 Beat lassi in a large bowl with an electric mixer until smooth. Return to container, cover; freeze a further 3 hours or until firm. (Alternatively, churn lassi in an ice-cream machine according to the manufacturer's instructions.)
5 Serve scoops of frozen lassi with extra peach slices and extra rind.

nutritional count per serving 0.8g total fat (0.5g saturated fat); 679kJ (162 cal); 30.2g carbohydrate; 6.8g protein; 2.1g fibre

tip If you have a zesting tool, use this to make thin strips of lime rind for serving.

GLUTEN FREE · DAIRY FREE · NUT FREE

BASIC VANILLA CUPCAKES

PREP + COOK TIME 45 MINUTES (+ COOLING) MAKES 14

Preheat oven to 180°C/350°F. Line 14 holes of two 12-hole (⅓-cup/80ml) muffin pans with paper cases. Beat 1 cup caster (superfine) sugar, 1 teaspoon vanilla extract and 3 eggs in a small bowl with an electric mixer for 5 minutes or until thick and pale. Add 125g (4 ounces) dairy-free spread, a little at a time, beating well between additions. Gradually add 1½ cups sifted gluten-free self-raising flour, ½ cup baby rice cereal (farex) and ¼ cup soy milk. Spoon mixture into paper cases. Bake 20 minutes. Stand for 5 minutes before turning, top-side up, onto a wire rack to cool. Make vanilla frosting (see right); spread frosting over cupcakes.

nutritional count per cupcake 13.9g total fat (3.4g saturated fat); 1250kJ (299 cal); 43.2g carbohydrate; 1.9g protein; 0.1g fibre

VANILLA FROSTING

BEAT 125G (4 OUNCES) DAIRY-FREE SPREAD AND 1 TEASPOON VANILLA EXTRACT IN A SMALL BOWL WITH AN ELECTRIC MIXER UNTIL PALE. BEAT IN 1½ CUPS SIFTED GLUTEN-FREE ICING SUGAR (PURE CONFECTIONERS' SUGAR) AND 2 TEASPOONS SOY MILK, IN TWO BATCHES, UNTIL WELL COMBINED AND SMOOTH.

GLUTEN FREE · DAIRY FREE · NUT FREE

BLUEBERRY CUPCAKES

PREP + COOK TIME 40 MINUTES (+ COOLING) **MAKES** 14

Preheat oven to 180°C/350°F. Line 14 holes of two 12-hole (⅓-cup/80ml) muffin pans with paper cases. Make one batch of basic vanilla cupcake mixture (recipe page 146); stir in ¾ cup frozen blueberries after adding the soy milk. Spoon mixture into paper cases. Bake for 20 minutes. Stand for 5 minutes before transferring, top-side up, to a wire rack to cool. Dust with gluten-free icing sugar (pure confectioners' sugar), if you like, or decorate with the vanilla frosting on page 146, or your favourite icing or ganache.

nutritional count per cupcake 7.6g total fat (1.9g saturated fat); 793kJ (189 cal); 29.1g carbohydrate; 1.9g protein; 0.2g fibre

THE CUPCAKES ON THESE TWO PAGES ARE BEST SERVED ON THE DAY OF BAKING. FREEZE UNICED CAKES IN AN AIRTIGHT CONTAINER FOR UP TO 3 MONTHS.

SWEET

GLUTEN FREE • EGG FREE • YEAST FREE • NUT FREE

BLUEBERRY AND WHITE CHOCOLATE SCONES

PREP + COOK TIME 30 MINUTES   MAKES 16

You need a 5cm (2-inch) round cutter.

3 cups (405g) gluten-free self-raising flour

1 tablespoon caster (superfine) sugar

2 teaspoons gluten-free baking powder

125g (4 ounces) fresh blueberries

180g (5½ ounces) white chocolate, chopped coarsely

1¼ cups (310ml) milk

1 tablespoon gluten-free icing sugar (pure confectioners' sugar)

⅓ cup (80g) blueberry jam

½ cup (125ml) crème fraîche

1 Preheat oven to 220°C/425°F. Line a baking tray with baking paper.
2 Combine sifted flour, sugar and baking powder in a large bowl. Add blueberries and chocolate; stir to combine. Make a well in the centre, add milk; stir until just combined.
3 Turn dough onto a lightly gluten-free floured surface; pat out until 3cm (1¼ inches) thick. Cut out 5cm (2-inch) rounds. Place scones, just touching, on tray. Gently knead scraps of dough together; repeat process.
4 Bake scones for 15 minutes or until browned lightly and cooked through. Dust with sifted icing sugar; serve immediately with jam and crème fraîche.

nutritional count per scone 7.3g total fat (4.6g saturated fat); 898kJ (214 cal); 35.5g carbohydrate; 2g protein; 0.3g fibre

tips Depending on the brand of flour you use, you may need to add extra flour. The scone dough should feel soft and slightly sticky to the touch. These scones are best served on the day they are made and are best eaten warm. You can use your favourite jam to serve with the scones.

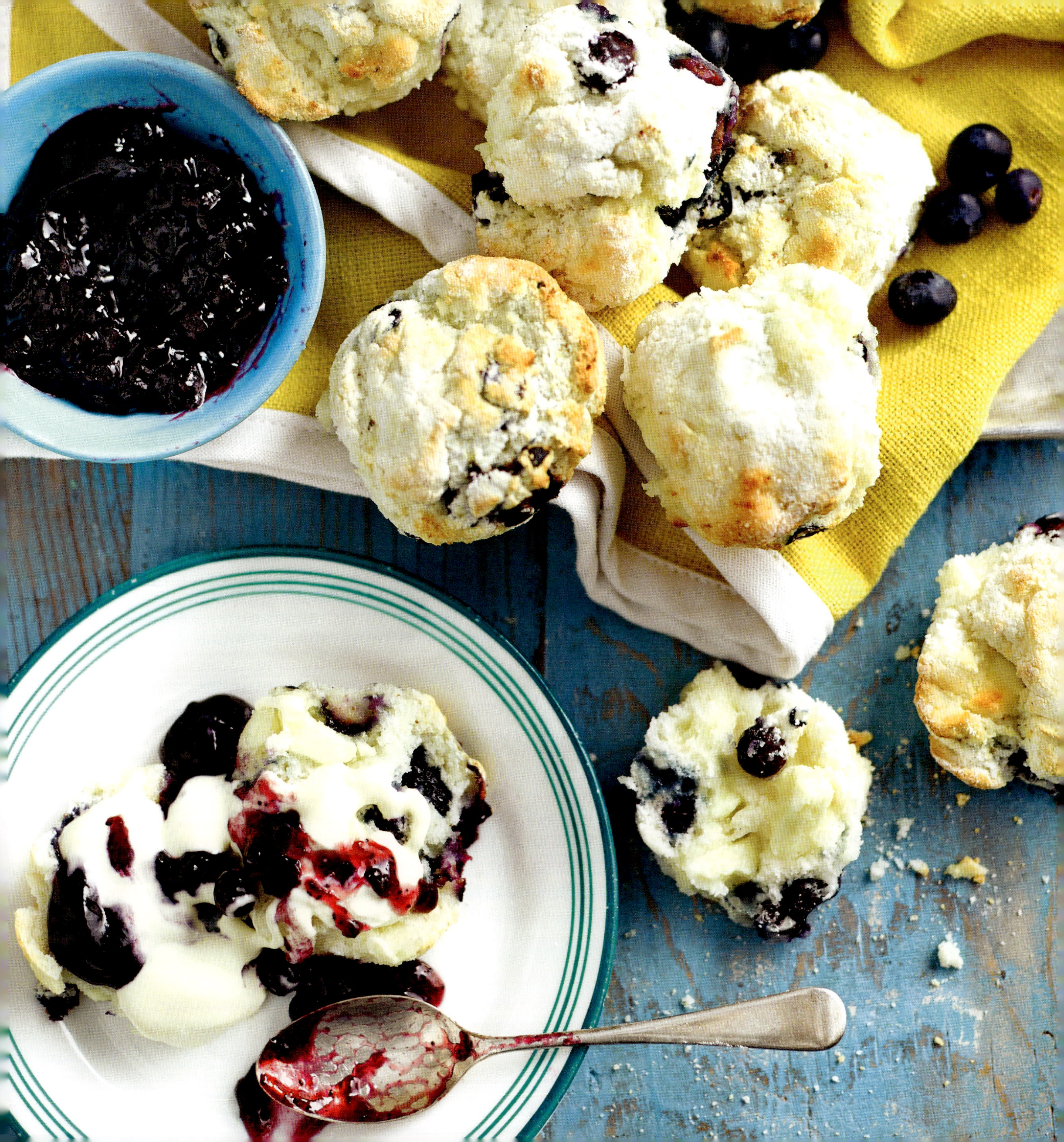

THE CAKE IS BEST SERVED ON THE DAY OF BAKING. REHEAT COLD CAKE SLICES IN A MICROWAVE OVEN ON MEDIUM (50%) UNTIL HEATED THROUGH.

SWEET

GLUTEN FREE • DAIRY FREE • NUT FREE

RASPBERRY AND LEMON SYRUP CAKE

PREP + COOK TIME 1¼ HOURS SERVES 8

dairy-free spread, for greasing
rice flour, for dusting
125g (4 ounces) dairy-free spread
¾ cup (165g) caster (superfine) sugar
1 tablespoon finely grated lemon rind
3 eggs, beaten lightly
1¾ cups (235g) gluten-free self-raising flour
¼ cup (60ml) soy milk
¾ cup (100g) frozen raspberries

LEMON SYRUP
1 tablespoon finely grated lemon rind
½ cup (110g) caster (superfine) sugar
¼ cup (60ml) lemon juice
¼ cup (60ml) water

1 Preheat oven to 190°C/375°F. Grease a 21cm (8½-inch) baba pan well with dairy-free spread; dust with rice flour, shake out excess.
2 Beat dairy-free spread, sugar and rind in a medium bowl with an electric mixer until light and fluffy. Beat in eggs, one at a time, until just combined. Stir in sifted flour and milk, alternately, in batches. Stir in raspberries. Spread mixture into pan.
3 Bake cake about 45 minutes.
4 Just before cake is cooked, make lemon syrup.
5 Stand cake in pan for 5 minutes before turning onto a wire rack over a tray. Pour hot syrup over hot cake.

LEMON SYRUP Stir ingredients in a small saucepan over heat, without boiling, until sugar dissolves. Bring to the boil. Reduce heat; simmer, uncovered, without stirring, for 5 minutes or until syrup thickens slightly.

nutritional count per serving 13.3g total fat (3.3g saturated fat; 1570kJ (375 cal); 61g carbohydrate; 3.6g protein; 1g fibre

tip If you have a zesting tool, use this to make thin strips of lime rind for serving.

serving suggestion Serve with vanilla soy ice-cream or vanilla bean soy yoghurt.

SWEET

GLUTEN FREE • EGG FREE • YEAST FREE • NUT FREE
CHOCOLATE CARAMEL SLICE

PREP + COOK TIME 40 MINUTES (+ COOLING) MAKES 20

⅔ cup (90g) gluten-free plain (all-purpose) flour
⅓ cup (75g) firmly packed brown sugar
⅓ cup (25g) desiccated coconut
85g (3 ounces) butter, melted
395g (12½ ounces) canned sweetened condensed milk
1 tablespoon golden syrup
40g (1½ ounces) butter, extra
150g (4½ ounces) dark (semi-sweet) chocolate, chopped coarsely

1 Preheat oven to 180°C/350°F. Grease a 19cm (8-inch) square cake pan; line base and sides with baking paper, extending the paper 5cm (2 inches) above sides.
2 Combine sifted flour, sugar and coconut in a medium bowl; stir in melted butter until combined. Spoon into pan; use the back of a spoon to press mixture evenly over base of pan.
3 Bake base for 15 minutes or until golden. Cool.
4 Place condensed milk, syrup and half of the extra butter in a medium saucepan; cook over medium heat, stirring constantly, for 10 minutes or until caramel is thickened and a golden colour. Pour over base; cool in pan.
5 Place chocolate and remaining extra butter in a medium heatproof bowl over a medium saucepan of simmering water (don't let water touch base of bowl); stir until chocolate melts. Pour chocolate mixture over caramel layer. Cool slice completely before cutting.

nutritional count per serving 10.4g total fat (6.8g saturated fat); 873kJ (209 cal); 27.4g carbohydrate; 2.7g protein; 0.3g fibre

tips Make an upside-down caramel slice by adding 2 tablespoons of cocoa powder to the biscuit base and replacing the dark chocolate with white chocolate. The slice can be made 1 week ahead; store covered in the fridge.

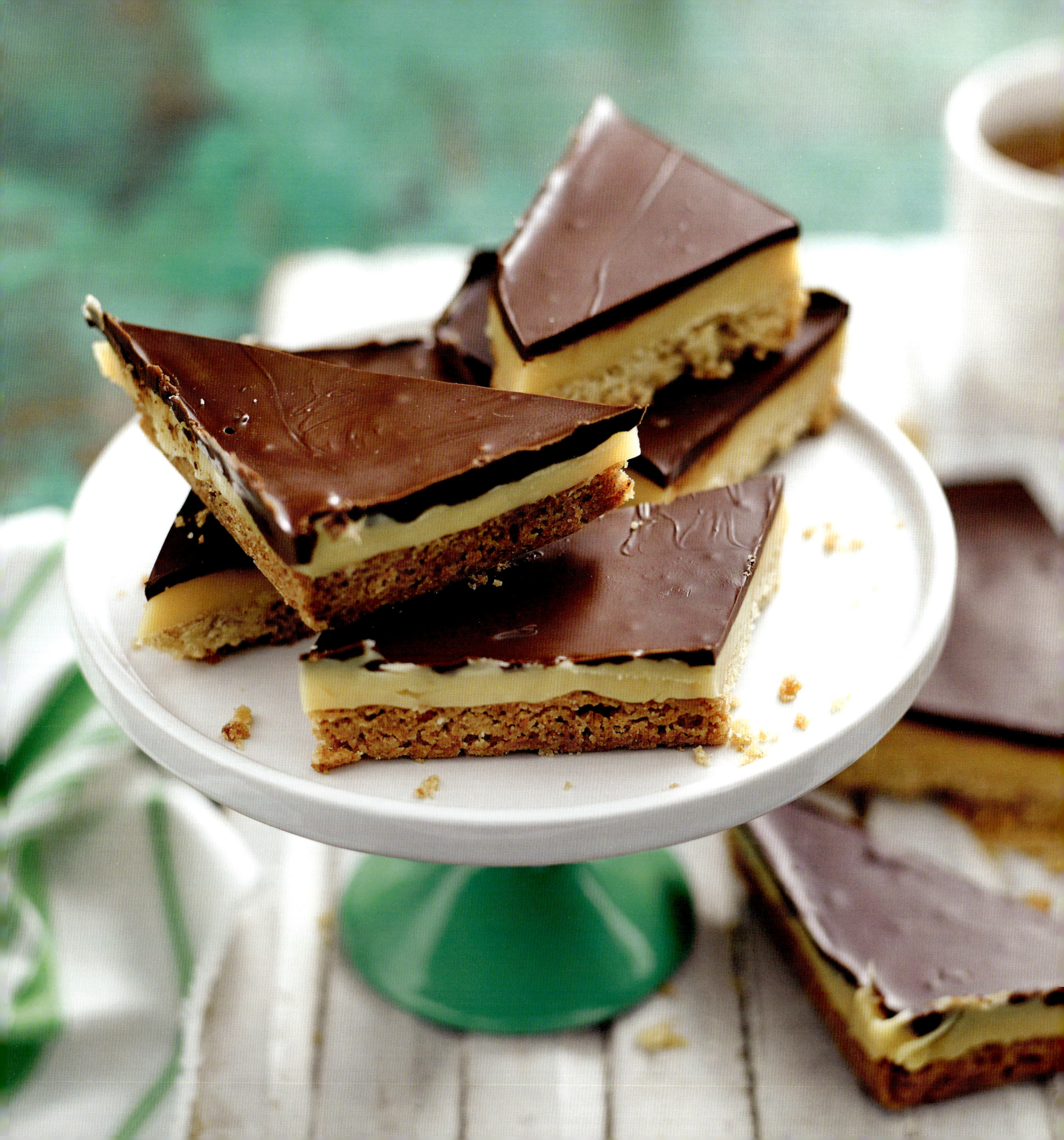

STORE SHORTBREAD IN AN AIRTIGHT CONTAINER IN THE FRIDGE FOR UP TO 2 WEEKS. SWAP PASSIONFRUIT FOR 2 TEASPOONS OF FINELY GRATED LEMON OR ORANGE RIND FOR A CITRUS-FLAVOURED SHORTBREAD.

GLUTEN FREE • EGG FREE • NUT FREE

PASSIONFRUIT SHORTBREAD WITH PASSIONFRUIT GLAZE

PREP + COOK TIME 1 HOUR MAKES 36

You need a 5cm (2-inch) heart-shaped cutter.

125g (4 ounces) cold butter, chopped coarsely

¼ cup (55g) caster (superfine) sugar

¾ cup (75g) rice flour

¾ cup (80g) gluten-free plain (all-purpose) flour

2 tablespoons gluten-free icing sugar (pure confectioners' sugar)

1 tablespoon xanthum gum

1 tablespoon passionfruit pulp

PASSIONFRUIT GLAZE

1 teaspoon (5g) softened butter

½ cup (80g) gluten-free icing sugar (pure confectioners' sugar)

2 tablespoons passionfruit pulp

1 Preheat oven to 150°C/300°F. Grease two oven trays; line with baking paper.
2 Beat butter and caster sugar in a small bowl of an electric mixer until just combined; gradually beat in the combined sifted flours, icing sugar and xanthum gum. Stir in passionfruit pulp.
3 Turn dough onto a lightly rice-floured surface; knead until just smooth. Roll out dough until 5mm (¼ inch) thick; using the heart cutter, cut 36 hearts from dough. Place hearts, about 2.5cm (1 inch) apart, on trays.
4 Bake shortbread for 15 minutes or until browned lightly and just firm. Stand on trays for 5 minutes before transferring to wire racks to cool.
5 Meanwhile, make passionfruit glaze.
6 Spread one side of the hearts with passionfruit glaze. Stand on wire racks until set.

PASSIONFRUIT GLAZE Stir ingredients in a small bowl until smooth.

nutritional count per shortbread 3g total fat (2g saturated fat); 251kJ (60 cal); 8.1g carbohydrate; 0.2g protein; 0.3g fibre

GLUTEN FREE · DAIRY FREE · NUT FREE

COCONUT CHERRY CUPCAKES

PREP + COOK TIME 45 MINUTES (+ COOLING) **MAKES** 14

Preheat oven to 180°C/350°F. Line 14 holes of two 12-hole (⅓-cup/80ml) muffin pans with paper cases. Make one batch of basic vanilla cupcake mixture (recipe page 146); stir in ¼ cup desiccated coconut, ½ cup sifted cocoa powder and ¼ cup soy milk into the mixture after adding the baby rice cereal (farex). Stir in 100g (3 ounces) finely chopped red glacé cherries and ¼ cup finely chopped dairy-free dark chocolate. Spoon mixture into paper cases. Bake for 20 minutes. Stand in pan 5 minutes before transferring, top-side up, to a wire rack to cool. Make vanilla frosting (recipe page 146), with the following changes: Combine 1 cup sifted gluten-free icing sugar (pure confectioners' sugar) and ½ cup sifted cocoa powder; beat combined sifted mixture with the 2 teaspoons of soy milk, in two batches, until combined and smooth. Spread over cupcakes.

nutritional count per cupcake 16.9g total fat (5.3g saturated fat); 1454kJ (347 cal); 46.3g carbohydrate; 3.4g protein; 2.1g fibre

THE CUPCAKES ON THESE TWO PAGES ARE BEST SERVED ON THE DAY OF BAKING. FREEZE UNICED CAKES IN AN AIRTIGHT CONTAINER FOR UP TO 3 MONTHS.

GLUTEN FREE · DAIRY FREE · NUT FREE

APPLE CINNAMON CUPCAKES

PREP + COOK TIME 30 MINUTES (+ COOLING) **MAKES** 14

Preheat oven to 180°C/350°F. Line 14 holes of two 12-hole (⅓-cup/80ml) muffin pans with paper cases. Make one batch of basic vanilla cupcake mixture (recipe page 146); stir in ⅓ cup canned pie apple into the mixture after adding the soy milk. Spoon mixture into paper cases. Bake for 20 minutes. Stand for 5 minutes before transferring, top-side up, to a wire rack to cool. Combine 2 teaspoons ground cinnamon and 2 tablespoons gluten-free icing sugar (pure confectioners' sugar); dust cupcakes with cinnamon mixture.

nutritional count per cupcake 7.6g total fat (1.9g saturated fat); 812kJ (194 cal); 30.4g carbohydrate; 1.8g protein; 0.3g fibre

SWEET

GLUTEN FREE • EGG FREE • NUT FREE

RASPBERRY AND VANILLA YOGHURT ICE-BLOCKS

PREP + COOK TIME 25 MINUTES (+ COOLING & FREEZING) MAKES 14

¼ cup (55g) low-GI cane sugar

1 vanilla bean, split lengthways

¾ cup (180ml) water

300g (9½ ounces) frozen raspberries

750g (1½ pounds) low-fat gluten-free plain yoghurt

1 Stir sugar, vanilla bean and the water in a small saucepan over low heat for 4 minutes or until sugar is dissolved. Bring to the boil without stirring. Reduce heat; simmer for 10 minutes or until syrupy. Remove vanilla bean; cool syrup.

2 Blend cooled syrup and raspberries until smooth. Very gently swirl in yoghurt. Pour mixture into 14 x ⅓ cup (80ml) ice-block moulds. Freeze overnight or until firm.

nutritional count per ice-block 0.2g total fat (0.1g saturated fat); 229kJ (55 cal); 8.3g carbohydrate; 3.5g protein; 1.3g fibre

Don't stir the yoghurt into the raspberry mixture or you will lose the marbled effect. It will swirl naturally when you pour the mixture into the moulds. Use a skewer to swirl it once in the moulds, if necessary. You could use frozen strawberries, cherries or mango.

SPECIAL OCCASIONS

BEFORE YOU START BASIC STEPS

LINING A ROUND CAKE PAN
Cut a strip of baking paper wide enough to line the side of the pan, extending below and above the side. Make a 2cm-fold on one long edge; snip at intervals to the fold. Cut a round of paper using the pan as a guide. Grease pan; place paper strip around side and round on base.

SEGMENTING AN ORANGE
Cut the top and bottom off the orange. Stand the orange on its flat base, then cut off the rind with the white pith following the curve of the fruit. Holding the orange over a bowl, cut down either side of each segment close to the membrane to release the fruit.

SPECIAL OCCASIONS

MAKING SUGAR SYRUP

Stir sugar and the water in a small saucepan, without boiling, until sugar dissolves. Brush down the sides of the pan with a wet pastry brush to remove any sugar crystals that start to form. Bring to the boil, without stirring, then simmer 10 minutes or until syrupy.

MAKING MERINGUE FROSTING

Beat egg whites in a small bowl with an electric mixer until soft peaks form. While the motor is operating, gradually pour the hot sugar syrup, in a thin steady stream, into the egg whites; beat on high speed for 10 minutes or until mixture is thick.

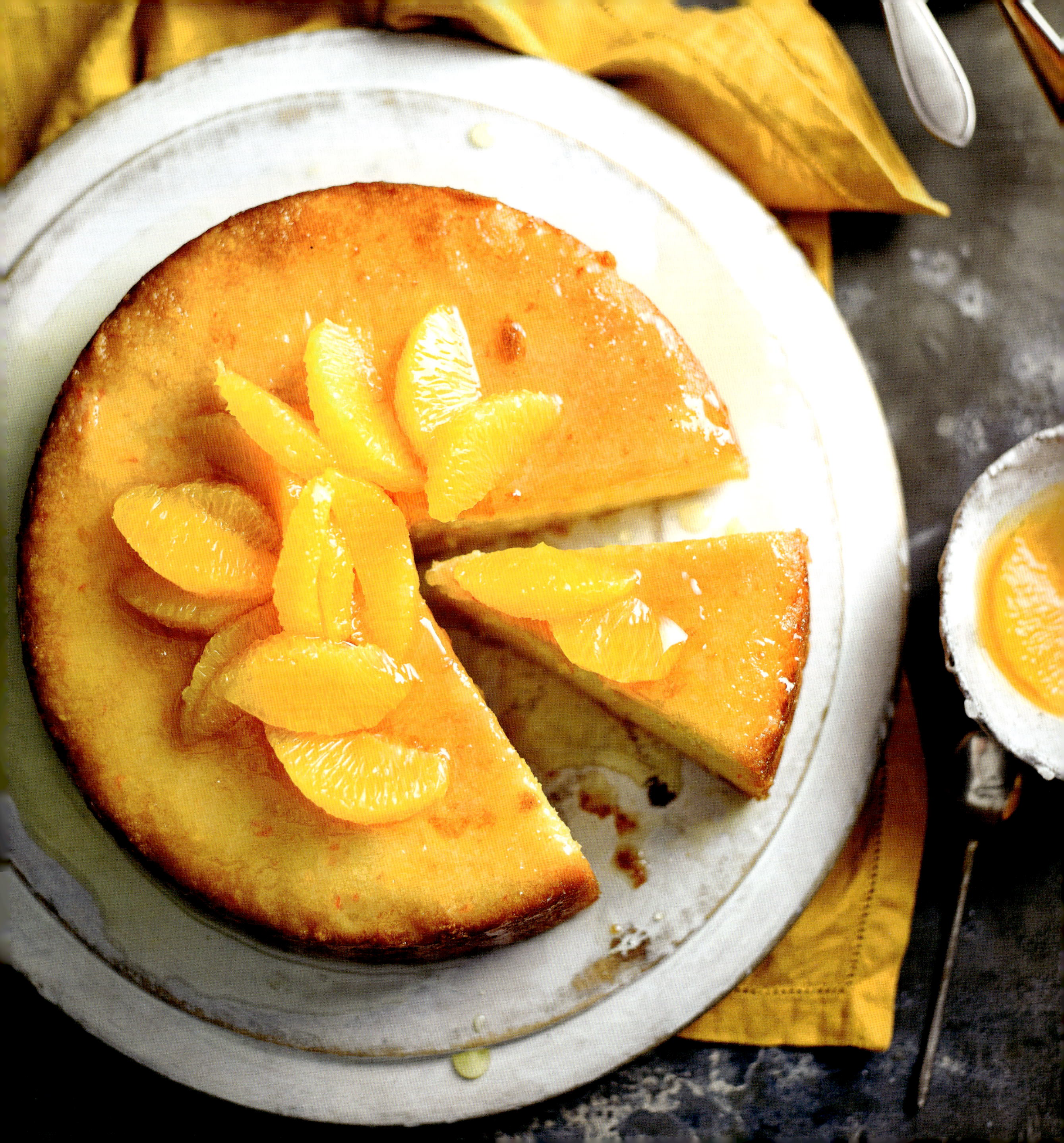

SPECIAL OCCASIONS

GLUTEN FREE • DAIRY FREE • NUT FREE

WHOLE ORANGE CAKE

PREP + COOK TIME 1½ HOURS (+ COOLING) SERVES 8

dairy-free spread, for greasing
2 large oranges (600g), unpeeled
3 eggs
1 cup (220g) caster (superfine) sugar
125g (4 ounces) dairy-free spread
1 cup (135g) gluten-free self raising flour
½ cup (65g) gluten-free plain (all-purpose) flour
¾ cup (50g) baby rice cereal (farex)

ORANGE SYRUP

1 cup (220g) caster (superfine) sugar
⅔ cup (160ml) orange juice
⅓ cup (80ml) water
3 medium oranges (720g), segmented (see tip)

1 Preheat oven to 180°C/350°F. Grease a deep 20cm (8-inch) round cake pan with dairy-free spread; line base and sides with baking paper.
2 Place unpeeled oranges in a medium saucepan; cover with water. Bring to the boil; boil, uncovered, for 2 minutes, drain.
3 Return oranges to same pan; cover with water and repeat step 2, two more times. Drain oranges; cool. Coarsely chop oranges; discard seeds. Blend or process rind and flesh until finely chopped.
4 Beat eggs and sugar in a small bowl with an electric mixer until thick and pale. Add dairy-free spread, a little at a time, beating well between additions. Gradually add sifted flours, rice cereal and 1½ cups of the processed orange (discard any remaining mixture). Spread mixture into pan.
5 Bake cake for about 50 minutes. Stand cake in pan for 5 minutes.
6 Meanwhile, make orange syrup.
7 Turn cake, top-side up, onto a wire rack over a tray; pour hot syrup over hot cake. Serve topped with reserved orange segments.

ORANGE SYRUP Stir sugar, juice and the water in a small saucepan, over medium heat, without boiling until sugar is dissolved; bring to the boil. Reduce heat; simmer, uncovered, without stirring, for 5 minutes or until thickened slightly. Stir in orange segments. Pour syrup into a heatproof jug; reserve orange segments.

nutritional count per serving 13.3g total fat (3.3g saturated fat); 2060kJ (492 cal); 89.4g carbohydrate; 4.6g protein; 2.9g fibre

tip To segment the oranges, cut off the rind with the white pith, following the curve of the fruit. Cut down either side of each segment close to the membrane to release the segment. (See also page 162.)

serving suggestion Serve with dairy-free ice-cream.

SPECIAL OCCASIONS

GLUTEN FREE • EGG FREE • YEAST FREE • NUT FREE
FRUIT MINCE PIES

PREP + COOK TIME 40 MINUTES (+ STANDING & COOLING) MAKES 24

The fruit mixture needs to marinate for 2 days. You need a 7cm (2¾-inch) round cutter and a 5cm (2-inch) star cutter.

⅔ cup (110g) sultanas

⅔ cup (110g) dried currants

⅔ cup (100g) raisins, chopped coarsely

⅓ cup (55g) mixed peel

⅓ cup (45g) dried cranberries

⅓ cup (50g) finely chopped dried dates

¼ cup (45g) finely chopped prunes

1 large apple (200g), peeled, grated coarsely

⅓ cup (75g) firmly packed brown sugar

¼ cup (85g) marmalade

2 tablespoons dark rum

½ teaspoon ground cinnamon

½ teaspoon mixed spice

1 roll (400g) packaged sweet vanilla bean gluten-free shortcrust pastry

2 tablespoons gluten-free icing sugar (pure confectioners' sugar)

1 Combine fruit, brown sugar, marmalade, rum and spices in a large glass bowl. Cover; stand at room temperature for 2 days, stirring occasionally.
2 Preheat oven to 180°C/350°F. Grease two 12-hole (1-tablespoon/20ml) shallow round-based patty pans.
3 Roll out pastry on a surface dusted with a little gluten-free flour until 3mm (⅛-inch) thick. Cut 24 x 7cm (2¾-inch) rounds from pastry, re-rolling scraps as necessary. Press pastry rounds into pan holes.
4 Roll remaining pastry scraps until 3mm (⅛-inch) thick. Cut 24 x 5cm (2-inch) stars from pastry re-rolling scraps as necessary.
5 Spoon 1 tablespoon of fruit mince into pastry cases; top with a pastry star.
6 Bake pies for 20 minutes or until browned lightly. Cool in pans. Dust with sifted gluten-free icing sugar.

nutritional count per pie 5.2g total fat (3.2g saturated fat); 776kJ (492 cal); 32.2g carbohydrate; 1.5g protein; 1.3g fibre

tips Sweet gluten-free shortcrust pastry comes in 400g (12½-ounce) cylindrical blocks; it is available in the freezer section of most major supermarkets. Mince pies will keep in an airtight container for up to 2 weeks.

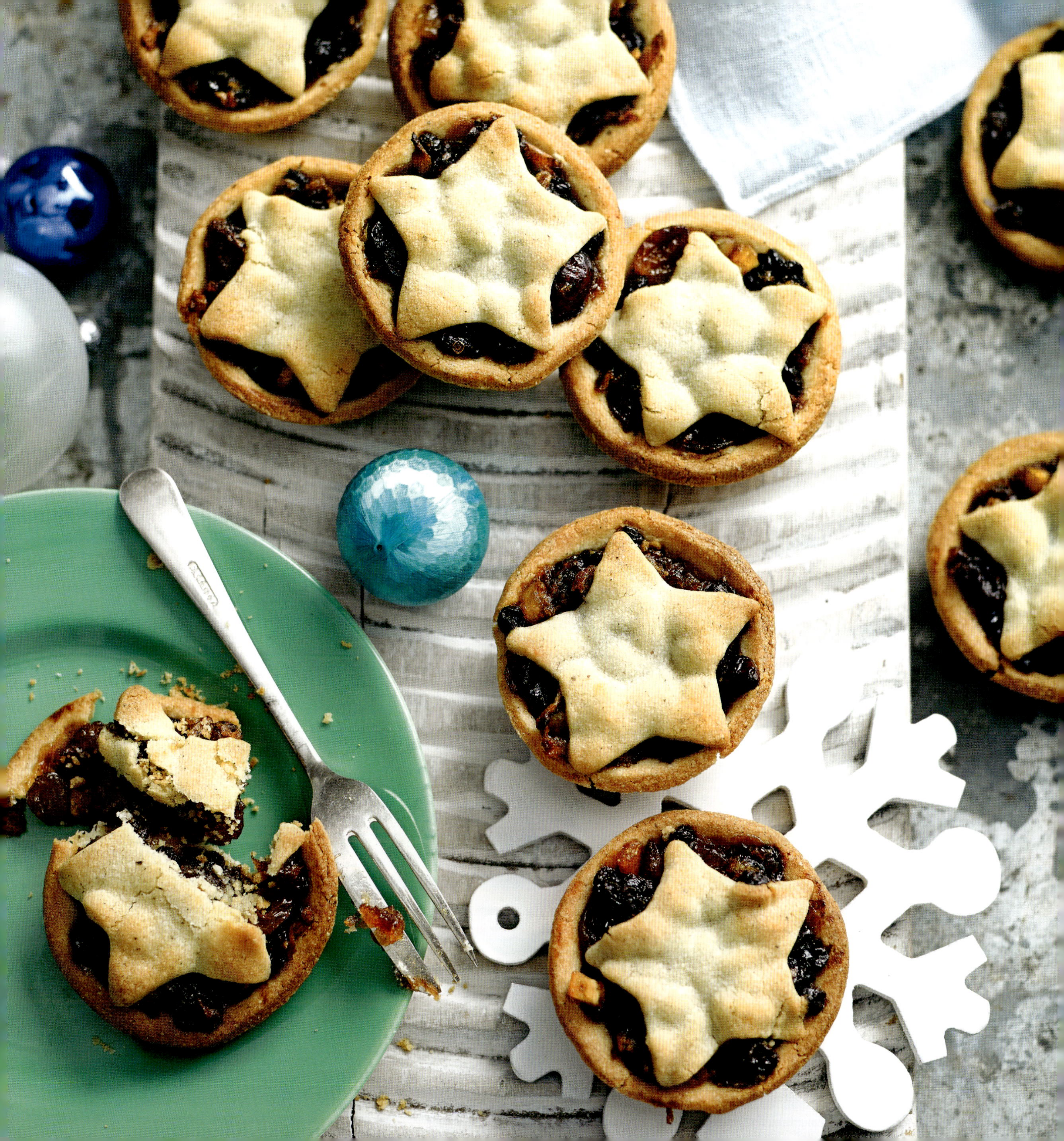

COVER THE CAKE WITH DARK CHOCOLATE GANACHE, IF YOU LIKE. THE CAKE CAN BE MADE 3 DAYS AHEAD; STORE, COVERED, IN THE FRIDGE. REMOVE CAKE FROM FRIDGE 2 HOURS BEFORE SERVING.

SPECIAL OCCASIONS

GLUTEN FREE • NUT FREE

CHOCOLATE MUD CAKE AND WHITE CHOCOLATE GANACHE

PREP + COOK TIME 1¾ HOURS (+ STANDING & COOLING)   SERVES 16

250g (8 ounces) butter, chopped coarsely
200g (6½ ounces) dark chocolate, chopped coarsely
2 cups (440g) caster (superfine) sugar
1 cup (250ml) milk
2 teaspoons instant coffee granules
1 cup (135g) gluten-free plain (all-purpose) flour
1 cup (135g) gluten-free self-raising flour
½ cup (90g) rice flour
¼ cup (20g) baby rice cereal (farax)
¼ cup (25g) cocoa powder
2 eggs

WHITE CHOCOLATE GANACHE
450g (14½ ounces) white chocolate, chopped coarsely
¾ cup (180ml) thickened (heavy) cream

1 Grease a deep 22cm (9-inch) round cake pan; line base and side with baking paper.
2 Stir butter, chocolate, sugar, milk and coffee in a large saucepan over low heat for 5 minutes or until chocolate melts and mixture is smooth. Remove from heat; cool for 5 minutes.
3 Whisk sifted flours, rice cereal and cocoa into chocolate mixture. Add eggs, whisk until combined. Pour mixture into pan; stand for 30 minutes.
4 Meanwhile, preheat oven to 160°C/325°F.
5 Bake cake about 1½ hours. Cool in pan.
6 Meanwhile, make white chocolate ganache.
7 Place cake on a serving plate or cake stand; spread ganache on top of cake.

WHITE CHOCOLATE GANACHE Place chocolate and cream in a small heatproof bowl over a small saucepan of simmering water (don't let water touch base of bowl); stir until chocolate melts and mixture is smooth. Refrigerate, stirring occasionally, for 30 minutes or until ganache is of a spreadable consistency.

nutritional count per serving 31.2g total fat (19.6g saturated fat); 2412kJ (576 cal); 71.3g carbohydrate; 5.4g protein; 0.7g fibre

SPECIAL OCCASIONS

GLUTEN FREE • DAIRY FREE • NUT FREE

STEAMED CHRISTMAS PUDDING

PREP + COOK TIME 7 HOURS (+ STANDING) SERVES 12

The fruit mixture needs to stand overnight.

750g (1½ pounds) dried mixed fruit
1 large green apple (200g), peeled, grated coarsely
½ cup (125ml) dry sherry
1 tablespoon finely grated orange rind
2 teaspoons mixed spice
1 teaspoon ground cinnamon
dairy-free spread, for greasing
125g (4 ounces) dairy-free spread
½ cup (110g) firmly packed brown sugar
2 eggs
2 cups (140g) stale gluten-free breadcrumbs
½ cup (65g) gluten-free plain (all-purpose) flour
½ cup (75g) tapioca flour

1 Combine mixed fruit, apple, sherry, rind, mixed spice and cinnamon in a large bowl. Cover with plastic wrap; stand at room temperature overnight.
2 Grease a 2-litre (8-cup) pudding basin or steamer. Line base with a small round of baking paper. Place a 30cm x 40cm (12-inch x 16-inch) piece of baking paper on top of a piece of foil cut to the same size; fold a 5cm (2-inch) pleat crossways through the centre.
3 Beat dairy-free spread and sugar in a small bowl with an electric mixer until pale. Beat in eggs, one at a time. Stir egg mixture into fruit mixture. Add breadcrumbs and combined sifted flours; stir to combine. Spoon mixture into basin; top with the pleated baking paper and foil (this allows pudding to expand as it cooks); secure with kitchen string (or the lid).
4 Place an inverted saucer in the base of a large saucepan; place pudding basin on the saucer. Pour enough boiling water into the pan to come halfway up the side of the basin; cover with a tight-fitting lid. Boil pudding for 6 hours, replenishing with boiling water as necessary to maintain water level.
5 Remove pudding basin from water. Stand pudding for 10 minutes before turning out. If you like, serve topped with dried figs and drizzled with golden syrup.

nutritional count per serving 8.3g total fat (1.9g saturated fat); 1547kJ (369 cal); 67.3g carbohydrate; 3.5g protein; 4.5g fibre

THE PUDDING CAN BE MADE 1 WEEK AHEAD; STORE, COVERED, IN THE FRIDGE, OR FREEZE FOR UP TO 3 MONTHS. TO REHEAT FROZEN PUDDING, THAW FOR 3 DAYS IN THE FRIDGE; REMOVE FROM FRIDGE 12 HOURS BEFORE REHEATING. DISCARD PLASTIC WRAP AND RETURN PUDDING TO PUDDING BASIN. STEAM FOR 2 HOURS FOLLOWING INSTRUCTIONS IN STEP 4.

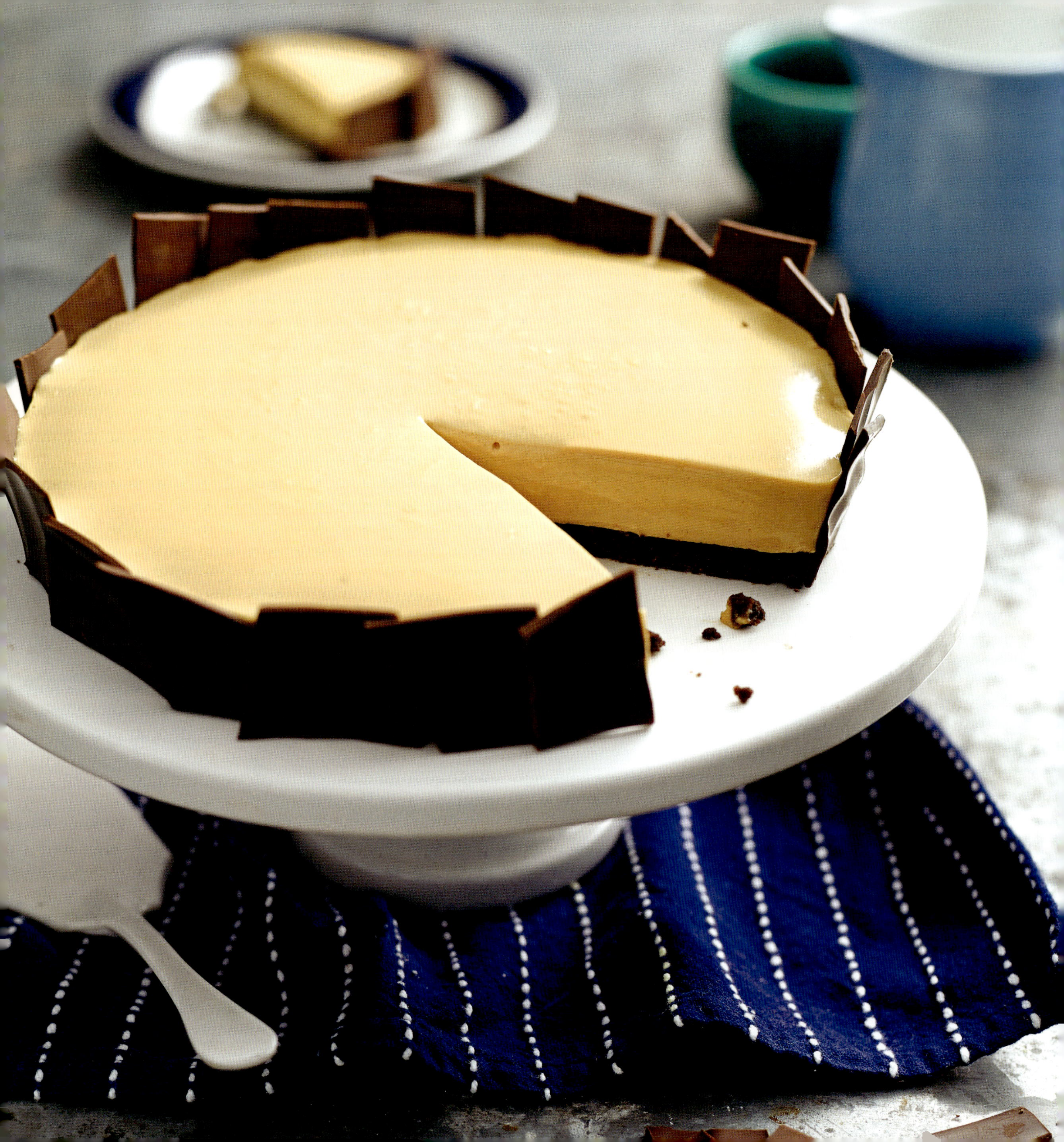

SPECIAL OCCASIONS

GLUTEN FREE • NUT FREE

CARAMEL CHOCOLATE CHEESECAKE

PREP + COOK TIME 45 MINUTES (+ REFRIGERATION & STANDING) SERVES 8

200g (5½ ounces) gluten-free plain chocolate biscuits

40g (1½ ounces) butter, melted

2 tablespoons golden syrup

1 teaspoon powdered gelatine

1 tablespoon water

250g (8 ounces) cream cheese, softened

¼ cup (60ml) thickened (heavy) cream

395g (12½ ounces) canned caramel top 'n' fill

1 cup (150g) dark chocolate Melts

1 Grease a closed 20cm (8-inch) (base measurement) round springform pan; line base with baking paper.
2 Process biscuits until fine; stir in butter and syrup until combined. Spread mixture evenly over base of pan. Cover; refrigerate 30 minutes.
3 Sprinkle gelatine on the water in a small heatproof jug. Stand jug in a small saucepan of simmering water; stir until gelatine is dissolved. Cool.
4 Beat cream cheese in a small bowl with an electric mixer until smooth. Add cream and caramel; beat until smooth. Stir gelatine mixture into cream cheese mixture; pour into pan. Refrigerate for 3 hours or overnight.
5 Place chocolate in a small heatproof bowl over a small saucepan of simmering water (don't let water touch base of bowl); stir until melted. Remove bowl immediately from heat. Spread chocolate on baking paper into a 20cm (8-inch) square; stand until set. Using a sharp knife, cut chocolate into pieces.
6 Remove cheesecake from pan to a serving plate. Press chocolate pieces around side of cheesecake.

nutritional count per serving 30.1g total fat (20.4g saturated fat); 224kJ (535 cal); 56.3g carbohydrate; 9.4g protein; 1.6g fibre

tips Use white chocolate Melts instead of dark chocolate, if you prefer. The cheesecake can be made 3 days ahead; store, covered, in the fridge. The chocolate pieces can be stored in an airtight container overnight. Press chocolate pieces around cheesecake just before serving.

SPECIAL OCCASIONS

GLUTEN FREE • DAIRY FREE • NUT FREE

LEMON MERINGUE CAKE

PREP + COOK TIME 1½ HOURS (+ COOLING & REFRIGERATION) SERVES 12

You need a sugar (candy) thermometer.

dairy-free spread, for greasing
3 eggs
¾ cup (165g) caster (superfine) sugar
1 tablespoon finely grated lemon rind
125g (3 ounces) dairy-free spread
1¾ cups (235g) gluten-free self-raising flour
¾ cup (180ml) soy milk
1 cup (320g) gluten-free lemon curd

MERINGUE FROSTING

1 cup (220g) caster (superfine) sugar
⅓ cup (80ml) water
3 eggs whites

CANDIED LEMON PEEL

2 medium lemons (280g)
¼ cup (55g) caster (superfine) sugar
¼ cup (60ml) water

1 Preheat oven to 180°C/350°F. Grease a deep 20cm (8-inch) round cake pan with dairy-free spread; line base and side with baking paper.
2 Beat eggs, sugar and rind in a medium bowl with an electric mixer until thick and creamy. Add dairy-free spread, a little at a time, beating until just combined. Gently whisk in sifted flour and milk, in batches, until smooth. Pour mixture into pan.
3 Bake cake for 45 minutes. Stand in pan for 5 minutes before turning, top-side up, onto a wire rack to cool.
4 Split cooled cake in half. Place one cake layer on a serving plate, cut-side up; spread with lemon curd, top with remaining cake layer. Refrigerate 30 minutes.
5 Meanwhile, make meringue frosting, then candied lemon peel.
6 Spread meringue frosting all over cake; decorate with candied lemon peel.

MERINGUE FROSTING Stir sugar and the water in a small saucepan over low heat, without boiling, until sugar dissolves. Bring to the boil; boil, uncovered, without stirring, for 10 minutes or until thickened slightly and reaches 116°C/240°F on a sugar (candy) thermometer. Syrup should be thick but not coloured. Remove from heat, allow bubbles to subside. Beat egg whites in a small bowl with an electric mixer until soft peaks form. While motor is operating, add hot syrup in a thin steady stream; beat on high speed for 10 minutes or until mixture is thick.

CANDIED LEMON PEEL Using a vegetable peeler, remove rind thinly from lemons; cut rind into long thin strips. Stir sugar, the water and rind in a small saucepan over low heat, without boiling, until sugar dissolves. Bring to the boil. Reduce heat; simmer, uncovered, without stirring, for 5 minutes or until mixture is syrupy.

nutritional count per serving 13.4g total fat (3.3g saturated fat); 1746kJ (417 cal); 72g carbohydrate; 3.8g protein; 0.2g fibre

THE CAKE CAN BE MADE A DAY AHEAD;
STORE, COVERED, IN AN AIRTIGHT CONTAINER.
ASSEMBLE JUST BEFORE SERVING.

Use your favourite ice-creams for this recipe. You can add chopped chocolate bars, jubes, marshmallows or coconut to the ice-cream. Dairy-free chocolate is free from milk solids; choose a 75% cocoa chocolate and always read the packaging labels to ensure the brand of chocolate you buy is actually dairy-free.

SPECIAL OCCASIONS

GLUTEN FREE • DAIRY FREE • EGG FREE • YEAST FREE • NUT FREE

COOKIES AND CREAM ICE-CREAM CAKE

PREP + COOK TIME 40 MINUTES (+ FREEZING, COOLING & REFRIGERATION)   SERVES 8

1 litre (4 cups) vanilla soy ice-cream

1 litre (4 cups) chocolate soy ice-cream

COOKIE DOUGH

125g (4 ounces) dairy-free spread

⅓ cup (75g) firmly packed brown sugar

⅓ cup (75g) caster (superfine) sugar

1¼ cups (210g) gluten-free plain (all-purpose) flour

½ teaspoon bicarbonate of soda (baking soda)

125g (4 ounces) dairy-free dark chocolate, chopped coarsely

1 Make cookie dough; refrigerate for 30 minutes.
2 Preheat oven to 200°C/400°F. Grease and line a baking tray with baking paper.
3 Using a quarter of the dough, roll tablespoons into balls; place balls on tray, about 2cm (¾-inch) apart. Bake for 20 minutes or until browned lightly and firm. Cool on tray.
4 Blend or process biscuits until fine; store in an airtight container until needed.
5 Line a deep 20cm (8-inch) round cake pan with plastic wrap.
6 Slightly soften vanilla soy ice-cream. Cut remaining cookie dough into chunks. Fold half the dough through the vanilla ice-cream; spoon into pan. Cover with foil; freeze for 30 minutes or until just firm.
7 Slightly soften chocolate soy ice-cream. Stir remaining cookie dough through chocolate ice-cream; spoon on vanilla ice-cream layer. Smooth surface, cover with foil; freeze for 3 hours or overnight.
8 Turn ice-cream cake upside-down onto a serving plate. Wipe side and base of pan with a warm cloth to release ice-cream from the pan; discard plastic wrap. Smooth ice-cream with a warm palette knife. Return to freezer for 30 minutes.
9 Just before serving, sprinkle top of ice-cream cake with reserved biscuit crumbs. Drizzle with extra melted dairy-free dark chocolate, if you like.

COOKIE DOUGH Beat dairy-free spread and sugars in a medium bowl with an electric mixer until pale. Beat in sifted flour and soda until smooth; stir in chocolate. Halve dough; wrap each half in plastic wrap.

nutritional count per serving 14.1g total fat (3g saturated fat); 1162kJ (397 cal); 64.6g carbohydrate; 3.4g protein; 3.2g fibre

SPECIAL OCCASIONS

GLUTEN FREE • DAIRY FREE • NUT FREE

CHRISTMAS FRUIT CAKE

PREP + COOK TIME 3 HOURS (+ COOLING) **SERVES** 12

dairy-free spread, for greasing

1kg (2 pounds) mixed dried fruit

½ cup (125ml) sweet sherry

250g (8 ounces) dairy-free spread

1¼ cups (250g) firmly packed brown sugar

½ cup (125ml) soy milk

1¼ cups (170g) gluten-free plain (all-purpose) flour

1 cup (65g) baby rice cereal (farex)

½ cup (75g) 100% corn (maize) cornflour (cornstarch)

½ teaspoon bicarbonate of soda (baking soda)

1 teaspoon ground cinnamon

3 eggs, beaten lightly

1 Preheat oven to 150°C/300°F. Grease a deep 20cm (8-inch) round cake pan with dairy-free spread; line base and side with three layers of baking paper, extending the papers 5cm (2 inches) above the side.
2 Combine fruit and half the sherry in a large bowl.
3 Stir dairy-free spread, sugar and milk in a medium saucepan over low heat until sugar is dissolved and spread is melted; pour over fruit mixture. Stir sifted dry ingredients into fruit mixture, in two batches, until combined. Stir in egg.
4 Spread mixture evenly into pan. Tap pan firmly on the bench to settle the mixture; smooth the surface.
5 Bake cake for 2½ hours or until cooked when tested (insert the blade of a sharp pointed knife gently through the centre of the cake to the bottom of the pan; gently withdraw the knife, there should be no uncooked mixture on the blade). If necessary, cover the cake with foil during cooking to prevent over-browning.
6 Brush hot cake with remaining sherry. Cover hot cake with foil; cool in pan overnight.

nutritional count per serving 17.4g total fat (4.1g saturated fat); 2244kJ (536 cal); 145.4g carbohydrate; 4.5g protein; 4.8g fibre

tips Replace the sherry with orange juice, if you prefer. The cake can be made up to 2 weeks ahead; store in an airtight container in the refrigerator, or freeze for up to 3 months.

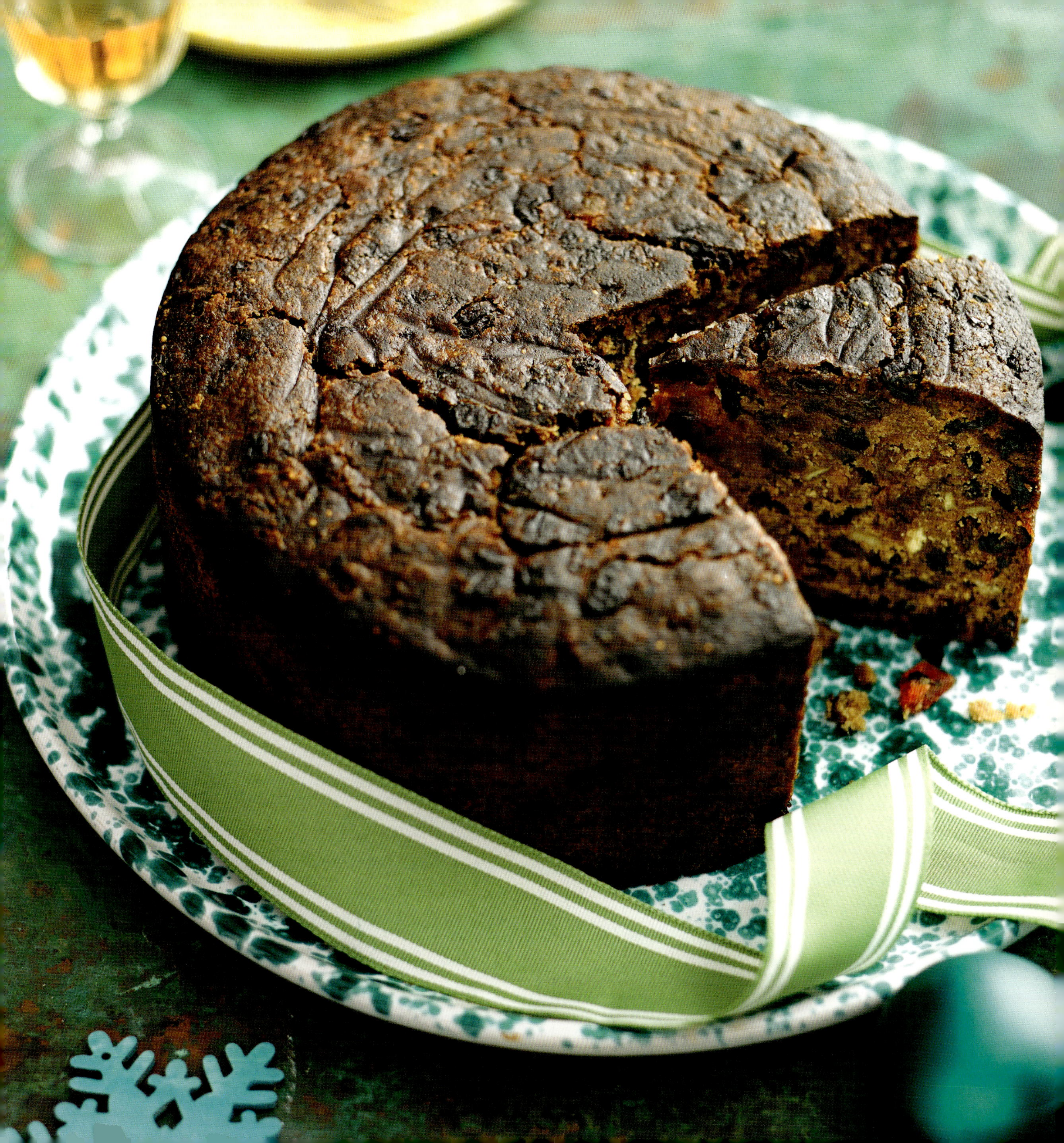

STAR INGREDIENTS

BLACK CHIA SEEDS
Contains protein and all the essential amino acids, making them a great addition to vegetarian and vegan diets.

WHITE CHIA SEEDS
Are nutritionally equal to black chia seeds; both are fibre-rich and provide a wealth of vitamins, minerals and antioxidants.

BROWN RICE FLOUR
Retains the outer bran layer of the rice grain. Contains no gluten. When cooked, it has a slightly chewy texture and nut-like flavour.

PUFFED RICE
This product is usually made by heating rice kernels under high pressure in the presence of steam.

POTATO FLOUR
Made from cooked, dehydrated and ground potato; it has a strong potato flavour and is a heavy flour so a little goes a long way.

CHICKPEA (BESAN) FLOUR
Also known as gram, this flour is made from ground chickpeas; it is gluten-free and high in protein.

LINSEED MEAL
Also know as flaxseed meal; available from the health food section in most major supermarkets.

BABY RICE CEREAL (FAREX)
Made from ground rice and sunflower oil; always check product labels as it may also contain traces of wheat, milk and soy.

XANTHUM GUM
A thickening agent made from fermented corn sugar; ensure the packaging clearly states this.

TAPIOCA FLOUR
This flour is made from the root of the cassava plant; it is a soft, fine, light white flour.

QUINOA
Pronounced keen-wa; is a gluten-free grain. It has a delicate, slightly nutty taste and chewy texture.

CORNFLOUR
This thickening agent is available in two forms: 100% corn (maize), which is gluten free and a wheaten cornflour (made from wheat) which is not.

QUINOA FLOUR
Made by grinding quinoa (pronounced keen-wa) into a powder; this flour is gluten-free and high in protein.

WHITE RICE FLOUR
A very fine, almost powdery, gluten-free flour; made from ground white rice.

GLUTEN-FREE PLAIN FLOUR
A blend of gluten-free flours and starches (may include, corn, tapioca, potato, chickpea and rice flours).

GLOSSARY

ALLSPICE so-named because it tastes like a combination of cumin, nutmeg, clove and cinnamon. Available whole or ground.

BAKING PAPER also called baking parchment or parchment paper; a silicone-coated paper primarily used to line baking pans and oven trays so cooked food doesn't stick.

BAKING POWDER, GLUTEN-FREE a raising agent; readily available from supermarkets.

BEETROOT also called red beets or beets; firm, round root vegetable.

BICARBONATE OF SODA (BAKING SODA) used as a leavening agent in baking.

BUTTER use salted or unsalted (sweet) butter; 125g is equal to one stick (4 ounces) of butter.

BUTTERMILK originally the term given to the slightly sour liquid left after butter was churned from cream, today it is made from no-fat or low-fat milk to which specific bacterial cultures have been added. Despite the implication in its name, it is actually low in fat.

CAPSICUM (BELL PEPPER) available in red, green, yellow, orange and purplish-black. Discard seeds and membranes before use.

CARAMEL TOP 'N' FILL a caramel filling made from milk and cane sugar. Can be used straight from the tin. Has similar qualities to sweetened condensed milk, only with a thicker, caramel consistency.

CARDAMOM a spice native to India and used extensively in its cuisine; available in pod, seed or ground form. Has a distinctive aromatic, sweetly rich flavour.

CAVOLO NERO also called tuscan cabbage, it is a staple in Tuscan country cooking. It has long, narrow, wrinkled leaves and a rich and astringent, mild cabbage flavour. It doesn't lose its volume like silver beet or spinach when cooked, but it does need longer cooking.

CHEESE
bocconcini from the diminutive of boccone meaning mouthful, is the term used for walnut-sized, baby mozzarella, a delicate, semi-soft, white cheese traditionally made in Italy from buffalo milk. Spoils rapidly so must be refrigerated, in brine, for 1 or 2 days at most.
cheddar the most common cow's milk 'tasty' cheese; should be aged, hard and have a pronounced bite.
fetta Greek in origin; a crumbly textured goat or sheep milk cheese with a sharp, salty taste.
haloumi a Greek Cypriot cheese with a semi-firm, spongy texture and very salty sweet flavour. Ripened and stored in salted whey; best grilled or fried, it holds its shape well on being heated. Eat while still warm as it becomes tough and rubbery on cooling.
mozzarella a soft, spun-curd cheese. It has a low melting point and an elastic texture when heated and is used to add texture rather than flavour.
parmesan also called parmigiano; is a hard, grainy cow-milk cheese originating in Italy.
pizza cheese a commercial blend of grated mozzarella, cheddar and parmesan cheeses.
ricotta a soft, sweet, moist, white cow-milk cheese with a low fat content and a slightly grainy texture. The name roughly translates as 'cooked again' and refers to ricotta's manufacture from a whey that is itself a by-product of other cheese making.

CHICKPEAS (GARBANZOS) also called hummus or channa; an irregularly round, sandy-coloured legume. Available canned or dried (soak in cold water before use).

CHOCOLATE
choc Bits also called chocolate chips and chocolate morsels; available in dark, milk, white and caramel. They hold their shape in baking and are ideal for decorating.
dairy-free dark buy a high-quality dark chocolate, which should only contain cocoa butter, cocoa liquor, lecithin (usually soy-based) and sugar. It should not contain any milk products; always check the ingredient label.
dark (semi-sweet) also called luxury chocolate; made of a high percentage of cocoa liquor and cocoa butter, and little added sugar. It is ideal for desserts and cakes.

GLOSSARY

Melts discs of compound chocolate ideal for melting and moulding.
white contains no cocoa solids but derives its sweet flavour from cocoa butter. Very sensitive to heat so watch carefully if melting.

CINNAMON available in pieces (called sticks or quills) and ground into powder; one of the world's most common spices.

COCOA POWDER or cocoa; dried, unsweetened, roasted then ground cocoa beans (cacao seeds).
dutch-processed is treated with an alkali to neutralize its acids. It has a reddish-brown colour, mild flavour, and is easy to dissolve in liquids.

COCONUT
desiccated concentrated, dried, unsweetened and finely shredded coconut flesh.
flaked dried, flaked, coconut flesh.
milk not the liquid inside the fruit (coconut water), but the diluted liquid from the second pressing of the white flesh of a mature coconut (the first pressing produces coconut cream). Available in cans and cartons at most supermarkets.
shredded unsweetened thin strips of dried coconut flesh.

CORN, PUFFED whole grain corn is steamed until it puffs up.

CORNFLOUR (CORNSTARCH) thickening agent available in two forms: 100% corn (maize), which is gluten free, and a wheaten cornflour (made from wheat) which is not.

CRANBERRIES, DRIED they have the same slightly sour, succulent flavour as fresh cranberries. Available in most supermarkets.

CREAM, THICKENED (HEAVY) a whipping cream that contains a thickener; it has a minimum fat content of 35%.

CRÈME FRAICHE mature fermented cream with a slightly tangy, nutty flavour and velvety texture. Used in savoury and sweet dishes. Minimum fat content 35%.

CUMIN a spice also called zeera or comino; has a spicy, nutty flavour.

CURRANTS dried currants tiny, seedless, almost black raisins so-named after a grape variety that originated in Corinth, Greece. Not the same as fresh currants.

DAIRY-FREE SPREAD made from vegetable oils; dairy-free substitute for butter.

EGGPLANT also called aubergine.

EGGS some recipes in this book may call for raw or barely cooked eggs; exercise caution if there is a salmonella problem in your area. The risk is greater for those who are pregnant, elderly or very young, and those with impaired immune systems.

FISH SAUCE also called nam pla or nuoc nam; made from pulverised salted fermented fish, most often anchovies. Has a pungent smell and strong taste; use sparingly.

FLOUR
brown rice retains the outer bran layer of the rice grain. Contains no gluten. It has a slightly chewy texture and nut-like flavour.
buckwheat not actually a form of wheat, but a herb in the same plant family as rhubarb; is gluten-free. Has a strong nutty taste.
chickpea (besan) also called gram; made from ground chickpeas so is gluten-free and high in protein.
gluten-free plain (all-purpose) a blend of gluten-free flours and starches (may include corn, potato, tapioca, chickpea and rice).
gluten-free self-raising made similarly to gluten-free plain flour, but with the addition of gluten-free bicarbonate of soda (baking soda).
potato made from cooked, dehydrated and ground potato; not to be confused with potato starch which is made from potato starch only. Potato flour has a strong potato flavour and is a heavy flour so a little goes a long way.
rice very fine, almost powdery, gluten-free flour; made from ground white rice.
tapioca made from the root of the cassava plant; a soft, fine, light white flour.

GELATINE we used powdered gelatine. It is also available in sheet form, known as leaf gelatine.

GHEE a type of clarified butter used in Indian cooking; milk solids are cooked until golden brown,

GLOSSARY

which imparts a nutty flavour and sweet aroma; it can be heated to a high temperature without burning.

GLUTEN is a combination of two proteins found in wheat (including spelt), rye, barley and oats. When liquid is added to the flour, these two proteins bind to become gluten. Gluten gives elasticity to dough, helping it rise and keep its shape; it also gives the final product a chewy texture.

GOLDEN SYRUP a by-product of refined sugarcane; pure maple syrup or honey can be substituted.

HONEY the variety sold in a squeezable container is not suitable for the recipes in this book.

KAFFIR LIME also known as magrood, leech lime or jeruk purut. The wrinkled, bumpy-skinned green fruit of a small citrus tree originally grown in South Africa and South-East Asia. As a rule, only the rind and leaves are used.

KAFFIR LIME LEAVES also called bai magrood, sold fresh, dried or frozen; looks like two glossy dark green leaves joined end to end, forming a rounded hourglass shape. Dried leaves are less potent, so double the number called for in a recipe if you substitute them for fresh. A strip of fresh lime peel may be substituted for each leaf.

LEBANESE CUCUMBER short, slender and thin-skinned. Probably the most popular variety because of its tender, edible skin, tiny, yielding seeds, and sweet, fresh and flavoursome taste.

LEMON CURD, GLUTEN-FREE a smooth spread, usually made from lemons, butter and eggs.

MAPLE SYRUP, PURE a thin syrup distilled from the sap of the maple tree. Maple-flavoured syrup or pancake syrup is not an adequate substitute for the real thing.

MILK
soy rich creamy 'milk' extracted from soya beans that have been crushed in hot water and strained. It has a nutty flavour.
sweetened condensed a canned milk product from which 60% of the water has been removed; the remaining milk is then sweetened with sugar.

MIXED BABY LEAVES also called salad mix or mesclun; a mixture of assorted young lettuce and other green leaves.

MIXED DRIED FRUIT a combination of sultanas, raisins, currants, mixed peel and cherries.

MIXED PEEL candied citrus peel.

MIXED SPICE a blend of ground spices usually consisting of cinnamon, allspice and nutmeg.

MUSHROOMS
button small, cultivated white mushrooms with a mild flavour.
dried porcini also known as cèpes; the richest-flavoured mushrooms. Expensive, but because they're so strongly flavoured, only a small amount is required.
flat large, flat mushrooms with a rich earthy flavour, ideal for filling and barbecuing. Are sometimes misnamed field mushrooms, which are wild mushrooms.
swiss brown also called roman or cremini. Light to dark brown mushrooms with full-bodied flavour; suited for use in casseroles or being stuffed and baked.

MUSTARD, DIJON pale brown, creamy, distinctively flavoured, fairly mild French mustard.

NUT-FREE BUTTER made from ground, roasted sunflower seeds; it's available in the health food section of supermarkets and online. A peanut-butter-like substitute for those with a peanut allergy.

OATS, GLUTEN-FREE read the package information to ensure these are grown and processed in an uncontaminated area. Oats contain gluten, and while some people with a gluten allergy may be able to tolerate oats, others will suffer a reaction. Anyone with a gluten allergy should check with a medical practitioner before eating any food containing oats.

OIL
cooking spray we use a cholesterol-free cooking spray made from canola oil.
grapeseed is a good-quality, neutral vegetable oil; available from supermarkets.
olive made from ripened olives. Extra virgin and virgin are the best, while extra light or light refers to taste not fat levels.
vegetable sourced from plants rather than animal fats.

OLIVES
black have a richer and more mellow flavour than the green ones and are softer in texture. Sold either plain or in a piquant marinade.
pimento-stuffed green a green olive with a lively, briny bitterness containing a morsel of capsicum, which adds a flash of colour.

GLOSSARY

ONION
brown/white are interchangeable, however, white onions have a more pungent flesh.
green (scallion) also known as (incorrectly) shallot; an immature onion picked before the bulb has formed, with a long, bright green edible stalk.
red also known as spanish, red spanish or bermuda onion; a sweet-flavoured, large, purple-red onion that is particularly good eaten in raw salads.

PAPRIKA a ground, dried, sweet red capsicum (bell pepper); there are many grades and types available, including sweet, hot, mild and smoked.

PASTRY, GLUTEN-FREE made from a blend of gluten-free flours and starches (may include corn, rice, tapioca, potato starch, pea) and binding and raising agents. Available in health-food stores, and in the health-food section of most supermarkets.

PEPITAS (PUMPKIN SEEDS) are the pale green kernels of dried pumpkin seeds.

POLENTA also called cornmeal; a flourlike cereal made of dried corn (maize) sold ground in different textures; also the name of the dish made from it.

POMEGRANATE MOLASSES not to be confused with pomegranate syrup or grenadine which is used in cocktails; pomegranate molasses is thicker, browner and more concentrated in flavour, tart and sharp, slightly sweet and fruity. Buy from Middle Eastern food stores or specialty food shops.

POTATOES
kipfler (fingerling) small, finger-shaped, nutty flavour; great baked and in salads.
sebago white skin, oval; good fried, mashed and baked.

QUINOA pronounced keen-wa; is the seed of a leafy plant similar to spinach. It has a delicate, slightly nutty taste and chewy texture.
flakes the grains have been rolled and flattened.
puffed that has been steamed until it puffs up.

RADISH a peppery root vegetable related to the mustard plant. The small round red variety is the mildest, it is crisp and juicy, and usually eaten raw in salads.

RAISINS dried sweet grapes.

RHUBARB has thick, celery-like stalks; the stalks are the only edible portion of the plant – the leaves contain a toxic substance. Though rhubarb is generally eaten as a fruit, it is a vegetable.

RICE CEREAL (FAREX), BABY made from ground rice and sunflower oil; always check the packaging as it may also contain traces of wheat, milk and soy.

RICE FLAKES is a dehusked rice which is flattened into flat light dry flakes. These flakes swell when added to liquid. The thicknesses of these flakes vary between almost translucently thin (the more expensive varieties) to nearly four times thicker than a normal rice grain. Easily digestible form of rice.

RICE, PUFFED usually made by heating rice kernels under high pressure in the presence of steam.

RICE, ROLLED flattened rice grains rolled into flakes; looks similar to rolled oats.

ROASTING/TOASTING nuts and dried coconut can be roasted in the oven to restore their fresh flavour and release their aromatic essential oils. Spread them evenly on an oven tray then roast in a 180°C oven for about 5 minutes. Pine nuts, sesame seeds and desiccated coconut toast more evenly if stirred over low heat in a heavy-based frying pan.

ROCKET (ARUGULA) also known as rugula and rucola; a peppery-tasting green leaf which can be used similarly to baby spinach leaves, eaten raw in salad or used in cooking. Baby rocket leaves, also known as wild rocket, are both smaller and less peppery.

SALAMI, GLUTEN-FREE DANISH cured (air-dried) sausages usually made with pork and beef. It has a mild smoky flavour and is blended with various herbs and spices.

SALMON, HOT-SMOKED a form of cooking whereby the smoke is circulated over the salmon for a short time at high temperature. This style of cooking results in a moist, subtly smoked salmon that flakes easily with a fork.

SILVER BEET also called swiss chard and mistakenly called spinach; a member of the beet family grown for its tasty green leaves and celery-like stems. Best cooked rather than eaten raw.

SPINACH also known as english spinach. Its thick, soft oval leaves and green stems are both edible. Baby spinach is also available.

GLOSSARY

SQUID also called calamari; a type of mollusc. Buy squid hoods to make preparation and cooking faster.

STERILISING JARS it's important your hands, the preparation area, tea towels and cloths etc, are clean. Always start with cleaned washed jars and lids, then follow one of these methods:
(1) Put the jars and lids through the hottest cycle of a dishwasher without using any detergent; or
(2) Stand the jars upright, without touching each other, on a wooden board on the lowest shelf in the oven. Turn the oven to the lowest possible temperature, close the oven door and leave the jars to heat through for 30 minutes.

Remove the jars from the oven or dishwasher with a towel. Stand the jars upright and not touching each other on a wooden board, or a bench covered with a clean towel to protect and insulate the bench. Fill the jars as instructed.

SUGAR
brown a very soft, fine granulated sugar retaining molasses for its characteristic colour and flavour.
caster (superfine) finely granulated table sugar.
gluten-free icing sugar (pure confectioners' sugar) also known as powdered sugar.
raw natural brown granulated sugar.

SULTANAS dried grapes, also known as golden raisins.

SUNFLOWER SEEDS grey-green, slightly soft, oily kernels.

TAHINI is a sesame seed paste available from Middle-Eastern food stores and some supermarkets.

TAMARI SAUCE a thick, dark soy sauce made mainly from soy beans and without the wheat used in standard soy sauce.

TOFUTTI a tofu-based dairy-free cream cheese substitute, available in the refrigerated section of health food stores and major supermarkets.

TOMATO
bottled pasta sauce a prepared sauce made of a blend of tomatoes, herbs and spices.
canned whole peeled tomatoes in natural juices; available crushed, chopped or diced. Use undrained.
cherry also called tiny tim or tom thumb tomatoes; small and round.
grape are about the size of a grape; they can be oblong, pear or grape-shaped and are often used whole in salads or eaten as a snack.
mixed medley contains a mix of grape, baby roma, Zebrino and cherry tomatoes. Each has a distinct shape, size and flavour with colours ranging from yellow, to red and brown with stripes.
paste triple-concentrated tomato puree used to flavour soups, stews, sauces and casseroles.
roma (egg) these are smallish, oval-shaped tomatoes used in Italian cooking or salads.
sauce (ketchup) a flavoured condiment made from tomatoes, vinegar and spices. Always check the packaging labels.

TURMERIC a member of the ginger family, its root is dried and ground, resulting in the rich yellow powder that gives many Indian dishes their characteristic colour. It is intensely pungent in taste but not hot.

VANILLA
bean dried, long, thin pod from a tropical golden orchid; the minuscule black seeds inside the bean impart a luscious flavour in baking and desserts.
extract made by extracting the flavour from the vanilla bean pod; the pods are soaked, usually in alcohol, to capture the authentic flavour.

VINEGAR
balsamic made from the juice of Trebbiano grapes; it is a deep rich brown colour with a sweet and sour flavour.
rice wine made from rice wine lees (sediment left after fermentation), salt and alcohol.
wine based on red wine.

WOMBOK (NAPA CABBAGE) also called chinese cabbage; elongated in shape with pale green, crinkly leaves, is the most common cabbage in South-East Asia. Can be shredded or chopped and eaten raw or braised, steamed or stir-fried.

XANTHAM GUM is a thickening agent produced by fermentation of, usually, corn sugar. When buying Xanthan gum, ensure the packet states 'made from fermented corn sugar'. Found in the health-food section in larger supermarkets.

YOGHURT
Greek-style plain yoghurt strained in a cloth (traditionally muslin) to remove the whey and to give it a creamy consistency.
soy an alternative to dairy yoghurt; usually an excellent source of calcium.

ZUCCHINI also called courgette.

CONVERSION CHART

MEASURES

One Australian metric measuring cup holds approximately 250ml; one Australian metric tablespoon holds 20ml; one Australian metric teaspoon holds 5ml.

The difference between one country's measuring cups and another's is within a two- or three-teaspoon variance, and will not affect your cooking results. North America, New Zealand and the United Kingdom use a 15ml tablespoon.

All cup and spoon measurements are level. The most accurate way of measuring dry ingredients is to weigh them. When measuring liquids, use a clear glass or plastic jug with the metric markings.

The imperial measurements used in these recipes are approximate only. Measurements for cake pans are approximate only. Using same-shaped cake pans of a similar size should not affect the outcome of your baking. We measure the inside top of the cake pan to determine sizes.

We use large eggs with an average weight of 60g.

DRY MEASURES

metric	imperial
15g	½oz
30g	1oz
60g	2oz
90g	3oz
125g	4oz (¼lb)
155g	5oz
185g	6oz
220g	7oz
250g	8oz (½lb)
280g	9oz
315g	10oz
345g	11oz
375g	12oz (¾lb)
410g	13oz
440g	14oz
470g	15oz
500g	16oz (1lb)
750g	24oz (1½lb)
1kg	32oz (2lb)

LIQUID MEASURES

metric	imperial
30ml	1 fluid oz
60ml	2 fluid oz
100ml	3 fluid oz
125ml	4 fluid oz
150ml	5 fluid oz
190ml	6 fluid oz
250ml	8 fluid oz
300ml	10 fluid oz
500ml	16 fluid oz
600ml	20 fluid oz
1000ml (1 litre)	1¾ pints

LENGTH MEASURES

metric	imperial
3mm	⅛in
6mm	¼in
1cm	½in
2cm	¾in
2.5cm	1in
5cm	2in
6cm	2½in
8cm	3in
10cm	4in
13cm	5in
15cm	6in
18cm	7in
20cm	8in
22cm	9in
25cm	10in
28cm	11in
30cm	12in (1ft)

OVEN TEMPERATURES

The oven temperatures in this book are for conventional ovens; if you have a fan-forced oven, decrease the temperature by 10-20 degrees.

	°C (Celsius)	°F (Fahrenheit)
Very slow	120	250
Slow	150	300
Moderately slow	160	325
Moderate	180	350
Moderately hot	200	400
Hot	220	425
Very hot	240	475

INDEX

A
apple cinnamon cupcakes 157

B
bacon, chive and potato quiche 109
basic steps, before you start
   chopping chilli 15
   cutting carrots into matchsticks 86
   greasing a baba pan 187
   hulling strawberries 14
   lining a round cake pan 162
   making meringue frosting 163
   making scones 136
   making sugar syrup 163
   melting chocolate 136
   preparing asparagus 85
   rolling out pastry 47
   segmenting an orange 162
   shallow frying schnitzels 84
   shaping gnocchi 84
   shredding wombok 46
   slicing fennel 15
   trimming beetroot 47
   trimming green onions 14
   trimming snow peas 46
   zesting citrus fruit 187
beef and rice stir-fry with carrot and cucumber pickle 126
beef pies 113
beetroot hummus and beef wrap 66
bircher muesli 41
blueberry and white chocolate scones 148
blueberry cupcakes 147
bread
   gluten-free 58
   raspberry and banana 38
breakfast
   bircher muesli 41
   breakfast wraps 28

(*breakfast* continued)
   buckwheat waffles with golden syrup 19
   buttermilk pancakes with lemon and sugar 24
   cinnamon funnel cakes 16
   crumpets with rhubarb compote 31
   granola with plums 32
   grilled eggs with spiced fennel and spinach 23
   ham and green onion fritters 20
   honey baked muesli 33
   maple glazed puffed corn 40
   omelette with asparagus and mint 37
   orange berry smoothie 43
   quinoa porridge with figs and raspberries 27
   quinoa porridge with grapes and pistachios 26
   raspberry and banana bread 38
   sausage, mushroom and roasted tomato rolls 34
   strawberries, hulling 14
buckwheat waffles with golden syrup 19
buttermilk pancakes with lemon and sugar 24

C
cakes
   caramel chocolate cheesecake 173
   chocolate mud cake and white chocolate ganache 169
   christmas fruit cake 178
   cinnamon funnel 16
   cookies and cream ice-cream cake 177
   lemon meringue 174
   raspberry and lemon syrup 151
   whole orange 165

caramel chocolate cheesecake 173
caramelised onion and spicy sausage pizza 122
carrot and cucumber pickle 126
char-grilled vegetables and pumpkin dip rolls 68
cheesy polenta fingers 53
cheesy rice balls with tomato chutney 65
chermoula tuna, chickpea and broad bean salad 79
chicken
   avocado and vegetable rolls 69
   family roast chicken and corn pie 110
   schnitzel with corn and tomato salad 90
   southern buffalo-style chicken wings 89
chilli dipping sauce 80
chocolate
   blueberry and white chocolate scones 148
   caramel chocolate cheesecake 173
   chocolate caramel slice 152
   chocolate mud cake and white chocolate ganache 169
   dark chocolate cheesecake brownie 142
christmas
   fruit cake 178
   steamed christmas pudding 170
chutney, tomato 65
cinnamon funnel cakes 16
coconut
   cherry cupcakes 156
   chicken and rice noodle salad 50
cookie dough 177
cookies and cream ice-cream cake 177
crêpes
   gluten-free 102

INDEX

(*crêpes* continued)
    pancetta and mushroom, with tomato sauce 102
crumpets with rhubarb compote 31
cupcakes
    apple cinnamon 157
    basic vanilla 146
    blueberry 147
    coconut cherry 156

D

dark chocolate cheesecake brownie 142
dinner
    bacon, chive and potato quiche 109
    beef and rice stir-fry with carrot and cucumber pickle 126
    beef pies 113
    caramelised onion and spicy sausage pizza 122
    chicken schnitzel with corn and tomato salad 90
    family roast chicken and corn pie 110
    gluten-free pastry 105
    gluten-free pizza dough 117
    jerk salmon with black bean salad 130
    mediterranean meatloaf 114
    mushroom, cavolo nero and quinoa risotto 129
    pancetta and mushroom crêpes with tomato sauce 102
    peanut-free satay chicken skewers 86
    potato and pumpkin gnocchi with rocket pesto 97
    puttenesca pizza 121
    roasted vegetables and bocconcini pizza 118

(*dinner* continued)
    salmon and quinoa kofta with herb tomato salad 94
    salmon parcels with kipfler potatoes 133
    salt and pepper squid 93
    sausage rolls 106
    smoked trout, pea and asparagus risotto 98
    southern buffalo-style chicken wings 89
    spicy lamb, spinach and fetta pizzas 125
    tandoori lamb cutlets with green onion roti 101

E

eggs
    grilled eggs with spiced fennel and spinach 23
    omelette with asparagus and mint 37

F

flour
    brown rice 180, 183
    buckwheat 183
    chickpea (besan) 180, 183
    cornflour 181, 183
    gluten-free plain 181, 183
    gluten-free self-raising 183
    potato 180, 183
    quinoa 181
    rice 183
    tapioca 181, 183
    white rice 181
food allergy 6–11
    diagnosis 10
    food intolerance, difference between 7–8
    how to manage 11

(*food allergy* continued)
    questionable testing methods 10–11
    statistics 6
    typical reactions to 9
    websites 11
    what is a 8
    whether increasing 7
food intolerance 8
    diagnosis 10
    food allergy, difference between 7–8
    questionable testing methods 10–11
    typical reactions to 9
    what is 8
fritters, ham and green onion 20
frozen peach lassi 145
fruit mince pies 166

G

ganache, white chocolate 169
glaze, passionfruit 155
gluten-free
    bread 58
    crêpes 102
    pastry 105
    pizza dough 117
    wraps 28
gnocchi, potato and pumpkin, with rocket pesto 97
granola with plums 32
grapeseed oil 184
green onion roti 101
grilled eggs with spiced fennel and spinach 23

H

haloumi, prosciutto-wrapped 57
ham and green onion fritters 20
herb tomato salad 94

INDEX

honey baked muesli 33
hot and sour prawn and
   chicken soup 76

I

ice-blocks, raspberry and
   vanilla yoghurt 158

J

jerk salmon with black bean
   salad 130

L

lamb
   tandoori lamb cutlets with
      green onion roti 101
lemon
   lemon meringue cake 174
   syrup 151
lemontons 138
lunch
   beetroot hummus and
      beef wrap 66
   char-grilled vegetables and
      pumpkin dip rolls 68
   cheesy polenta fingers 53
   cheesy rice balls with tomato
      chutney 65
   chermoula tuna, chickpea and
      broad bean salad 79
   chicken, avocado and
      vegetable rolls 69
   coconut chicken and rice
      noodle salad 50
   gluten-free bread 58
   hot and sour prawn and
      chicken soup 76
   mushroom and tomato tarts 54
   olive and bacon pizza scrolls 62
   pastrami with silver beet
      coleslaw 60
   prosciutto-wrapped haloumi 57
   quinoa salad with vegetables
      and tuna 71
   salmon and quinoa salad 48

(*lunch* continued)
   spiced lentil and roasted
      kumara soup 72
   tuna with quinoa tabbouleh 61
   turkey and brown rice salad 75
   vietnamese pancakes
      with prawns 80

M

maple glazed puffed corn 40
meatloaf, mediterranean 114
meringue frosting 163, 174
muesli
   bircher 41
   honey baked 33
mushrooms
   mushroom and tomato tarts 54
   mushroom, cavolo nero and
      quinoa risotto 129

O

olive and bacon pizza scrolls 62
omelette with asparagus and mint 37
orange
   berry smoothie 43
   filling 141
   syrup 165
   whole orange cake 165

P

pancakes
   buttermilk pancakes with
      lemon and sugar 24
   vietnamese, with prawns 80
pancetta and mushroom crêpes
   with tomato sauce 102
passionfruit glaze 155
passionfruit shortbread with
   passionfruit glaze 155
pastrami with silver beet coleslaw 60
pastry, gluten-free 105
peach lassi, frozen 145
peanut-free satay chicken skewers 86
pesto, rocket 97
pickle, carrot and cucumber 126

pies
   beef 113
   family roast chicken and corn 110
   fruit mince 166
pizza
   caramelised onion and spicy
      sausage 122
   gluten-free pizza dough 117
   olive and bacon pizza scrolls 62
   puttenesca 121
   roasted vegetables and
      bocconcini 118
   spicy lamb, spinach and fetta 125
porridge
   quinoa, with figs and
      raspberries 27
   quinoa, with grapes and
      pistachios 26
potato and pumpkin gnocchi
   with rocket pesto 97
prosciutto-wrapped haloumi 57
puffed corn, maple glazed 40
puttenesca pizza 121

Q

quiche, bacon, chive and potato 109
quinoa
   porridge with figs and
      raspberries 27
   porridge with grapes and
      pistachios 26
   salad with vegetables and tuna 71

R

raspberry and banana bread 38
raspberry and lemon syrup cake 151
raspberry and vanilla yoghurt
   ice-blocks 158
red velvet whoopie pies
   with orange filling 141
rhubarb compote 31
risotto
   mushroom, cavolo nero and
      quinoa 129
   smoked trout, pea and
      asparagus 98

INDEX

roasted vegetables and
   bocconcini pizza 118
rocket pesto 97
rolls
   char-grilled vegetables and
      pumpkin dip 68
   chicken, avocado and vegetable 69
   sausage 106
roti, green onion 101

S

salads
   chermoula tuna, chickpea
      and broad bean 79
   coconut chicken and
      rice noodle 50
   corn and tomato salad 90
   herb tomato 94
   jerk salmon with black bean 130
   quinoa, with vegetables
      and tuna 71
   salmon and quinoa 48
   silver beet coleslaw 60
   turkey and brown rice 75
salmon
   parcels with kipfler potatoes 133
   salmon and quinoa kofta
      with herb tomato salad 94
   salmon and quinoa salad 48
salsa, tomato avocado 89
salt and pepper squid 93
satay chicken skewers,
   peanut-free 86
sauce, chilli dipping 80
sausage, mushroom and roasted
   tomato rolls 34
sausage rolls 106
scones, blueberry and white
   chocolate 148
silver beet coleslaw 60
smoked trout, pea and asparagus
   risotto 98
smoothie, orange berry 43
soup
   hot and sour prawn and
      chicken 76

(*soup* continued)
   spiced lentil and roasted
      kumara 72
southern buffalo-style chicken
   wings 89
special occasions
   caramel chocolate cheesecake 173
   chocolate mud cake and white
      chocolate ganache 169
   christmas fruit cake 178
   cookies and cream ice-cream
      cake 177
   fruit mince pies 166
   lemon meringue cake 174
   steamed christmas pudding 170
   sugar syrup, making 163
   whole orange cake 165
spiced lentil and roasted
   kumara soup 72
spicy lamb, spinach and
   fetta pizzas 125
star ingredients
   baby rice cereal (farex) 181
   black chia seeds 180
   brown rice flour 180
   chickpea (besan) flour 180
   cornflour 181
   gluten-free plain flour 181
   linseed meal 181
   potato flour 180
   puffed rice 180
   quinoa 181
   quinoa flour 181
   tapioca flour 181
   white chia seeds 180
   white rice flour 181
   xanthum gum 181
steamed christmas pudding 170
stir-fry, beef and rice, with carrot
   and cucumber pickle 126
sweet
   apple cinnamon cupcakes 157
   blueberry and white chocolate
      scones 148
   blueberry cupcakes 147
   chocolate caramel slice 152

(*sweet* continued)
   coconut cherry cupcakes 156
   dark chocolate cheesecake
      brownie 142
   frozen peach lassi 145
   lemontons 138
   passionfruit shortbread with
      passionfruit glaze 155
   raspberry and lemon syrup
      cake 151
   raspberry and vanilla yoghurt
      ice-blocks 158
   red velvet whoopie pies
      with orange filling 141
   vanilla cupcakes, basic 146
syrup
   lemon 151
   orange 165

T

tandoori lamb cutlets with
   green onion roti 101
tarts, mushroom and tomato 54
tomato
   avocado salsa 89
   chutney 65
tuna with quinoa tabbouleh 61
turkey and brown rice salad 75

V

vanilla cupcakes, basic 146
vietnamese pancakes with prawns 80

W

waffles, buckwheat, with
   golden syrup 19
white chocolate ganache 169
whole orange cake 165
wraps
   beetroot hummus and beef 66
   breakfast 28
   gluten-free 28

Published in 2015 by Bauer Media Books, Australia
Bauer Media Books is a division of Bauer Media Pty Limited.

BAUER MEDIA GROUP

BAUER MEDIA BOOKS
Publisher Jo Runciman
Editorial & food director Pamela Clark
Director of sales, marketing & rights Brian Cearnes
Creative director Hieu Chi Nguyen
Art director Hannah Blackmore
Senior editors Wendy Bryant, Stephanie Kistner
Food editor Emma Braz
Designer Jeannel Cunanan
Senior business analyst Rebecca Varela
Operations manager David Scotto

Published by Bauer Media Books, a division of Bauer Media Pty Ltd,
54 Park St, Sydney; GPO Box 4088,
Sydney, NSW 2001, Australia.
phone +61 2 9282 8618; fax +61 2 9126 3702
www.awwcookbooks.com.au

Printed in China with 1010 Printing Asia Limited.

Australia Distributed by Network Services,
phone +61 2 9282 8777; fax +61 2 9264 3278;
networkweb@networkservicescompany.com.au

New Zealand Distributed by Bookreps NZ Ltd,
phone +64 9 419 2635; fax +64 9 419 2634;
susan@bookreps.co.nz

South Africa Distributed by PSD Promotions,
phone +27 11 392 6065/6/7; fax +27 11 392 6079/80;
orders@psdprom.co.za

A catalogue record for this book is available from the National Library of Australia.
ISBN: 978-1-74245-429-0

© Bauer Media Pty Limited 2015
ABN 18 053 273 546
This publication is copyright. No part of it may be
reproduced or transmitted in any form without the
written permission of the publishers.

Photographer John Paul Urizar
Stylist Vivien Walsh
Food preparation Sarah Hobbs
Recipe development Nadia French, Sarah Hobbs
Front cover Raspberry and lemon syrup cake, page 151
Back cover Lemontons, page 138

To order books
phone 136 116 (within Australia) or
order online at www.awwcookbooks.com.au
Send recipe enquiries to:
recipeenquiries@bauer-media.com.au